SAY IT IN
RUSSIAN

Revised and Enlarged Edition

by Michael S. Flier

Professor of Slavic Languages and Literatures
University of California, Los Angeles

DOVER PUBLICATIONS, INC.
New York

Für Elyse—when you're back in the U.S.S.R.

The Dover *Say It* series is prepared under the editorial supervision of R. A. Sorenson.

Published in Canada by General Publishing Company, Ltd., 30 Lesmill Road, Don Mills, Toronto, Ontario.
Published in the United Kingdom by Constable and Company, Ltd., 10 Orange Street, London WC2H 7EG.

This Dover edition, first published in 1982, is a completely revised and enlarged work, which supersedes the book of the same title originally published by Dover Publications, Inc., in 1954.

Manufactured in the United States of America
Dover Publications, Inc.
180 Varick Street
New York, N.Y. 10014

Library of Congress Cataloging in Publication Data

Flier, Michael S.
  Say it in Russian.

  (Dover "say it" series)
  Rev ed. of: Say it in Russian/N. C. Stepanoff. 1954.
  Includes index.
  1. Russian language—Conversation and phrase books—English. I. Stepanoff, N. C. Say it in Russian. II. Title.
PG2121.F53 1982   491.783′421   82-7292
ISBN 0-486-20810-9 (pbk.)   AACR2

TABLE OF CONTENTS

INTRODUCTION

Say It in Russian is based on Contemporary Standard Russian, the literary norm of the Russian language as spoken in the Soviet Union today. Although the standard language is based on the Central Russian dialect spoken in Moscow and differs in a number of respects from the spoken dialects of northern and southern Russia, it is readily understood by all Russian speakers and by most Soviet citizens whose first language is not Russian.

Russian is related to most of the languages of Eastern Europe. As a Slavic language, it falls into the East Slavic group along with Ukrainian and Belorussian (White Russian). The West Slavic group includes Czech, Slovak and Polish, while Bulgarian and Serbo-Croatian are among the South Slavic languages. The 1980 edition of *The World Almanac* estimates that there are 259 million speakers of Russian, a figure that places it third, after Mandarin Chinese and English, among the major languages of the world.

NOTES ON THE USE OF THIS BOOK

Say It in Russian is divided into sections by topics geared to various situations likely to be encountered by the traveler in the Soviet Union. Such topics include social conversation, travel, eating, shopping, health and illness. The entries in most sections are alphabetized according to their English headings; exceptions are the sections on food and public notices and signs, which are alphabetized according to the Russian to permit quick and easy reference.

In the extensive index at the end of the book, capitalized items refer to section headings and give the number of the page on which the section begins. All other numbers refer to the separate, consecutively numbered entries. The index itself serves as a useful English-Russian glossary; any word not in the section where you expect to find it is likely to be in the index.

Say It in Russian contains words, phrases and sentences likely to be essential for travel in the Soviet Union. This material will serve as an interesting introduction to spoken Russian if you plan to study the language, but will be useful whether or not you study Russian on a formal basis. With the aid of the index, a guidebook, or an English-Russian dictionary, many sentence patterns here will answer innumerable needs. For example, the slot occupied by "Red Square" in the sentence

How long does it take to walk to [Red Square]?

may be filled by any other word or phrase denoting a nearby destination, such as "Gorky Street" or "Hotel Rossiya."* In other sentences, the words in square brackets can be replaced with words immediately following (in the same sentence or in the indented entries below it). For example, the entry

Turn [left] [right] at the next corner.

provides two sentences: "Turn left at the next corner"

---

* Although the words you supply for the substitutions will not always be in the grammatically correct form, Russians should have no trouble understanding what is meant. (Because Russian is a highly inflected language, nouns, pronouns, adjectives, participles and verbs have different endings depending on their function in the sentence. Thus, one English word may be translated with different forms of its Russian equivalent depending on the context.)

and "Turn right at the next corner." Three sentences are provided by the entry

> Give me a seat [on the aisle].
> —by a window.
> —by the emergency exit.

As your Russian vocabulary grows, you will find that you can express an increasingly wide range of thoughts by the proper substitution of words in these model sentences.

A slash is used to separate alternative entries when an English word can be translated by Russian words which are not synonymous:

> Factory (heavy industry/light industry).
> Заво́д/Фа́брика.

Please note that while brackets always indicate the possibility of substitution, parentheses have been used to provide additional information. They are used to indicate synonyms or alternative usage for an entry:

> Hello (OR: Hi).

Occasionally, parentheses may be used to clarify a word or to explain something unfamiliar to English speakers (such as Russian foods). The abbreviation "(LIT.)" is used whenever a literal translation of a Russian sentence is provided. Parentheses are also used to indicate words that can readily be omitted:

> We forgot our keys.   Мы́ забы́ли (на́ши) ключи́.

The Russian word for "our" is often omitted from this phrase.

Parentheses also indicate different forms of the same

word that vary according to gender or number. Though it is not the purpose of this book to teach Russian grammar, parentheses are used to clarify grammatical points necessary for producing correct phrases. Nouns in Russian are either masculine (M.), feminine (F.) or neuter (N.). Adjectives, pronouns, participles and past-tense verbs also vary according to gender and whether they are singular (SG.) or plural (PL.). The entry "I am a student" is translated in either of two ways, depending on whether the speaker is male or female:

Я — студе́нт (F.: студе́нтка).
yah — stoo-DᵞEHNT (F.: *stoo-DᵞEHNT-kuh*).

Please note, too, that Russian has no articles (a, an, the) or, in most cases, present-tense forms of the verb "to be"; thus, you can produce sentences of this type without further study:

He is a doctor. Он — до́ктор. *ohn — DOHK-tuhr.*

The word "please" has been omitted from many of the sentences for reasons of space. To be polite, you should add пожа́луйста (*pah-ZHAH-lĭ-stuh*) whenever you would normally say "please" in English.

PRONUNCIATION

The explanatory chart of the simplified phonetic transcription system provided below will aid you in the correct pronunciation of Russian words. But the transcription is at best only an approximation of Russian sounds; ultimate precision and consistency have occasionally been sacrificed for simplicity and ease of comprehension. You will derive great benefit from listening to and repeating aloud recorded Russian speech as provided in the Dover *Listen & Learn* language recordings for Russian.

Russian, with rare exceptions, stresses only one syllable in each word; the vowels in unstressed syllables are subject to varying degrees of alteration in sound (discussed below). In our transcription system, syllables are separated by hyphens and the stressed syllable is printed in capital letters:

> Hand. Рука́. *roo-KAH.*
> Vodka. Во́дка. *VOHT-kuh.*

One-syllable words are not capitalized even when they bear normal word stress:

> Soup. Су́п. *soop.*

Most one-syllable Russian prepositions and particles do not carry their own stress; they are pronounced together with the words they precede or follow. In our transcription system they will either be joined directly to the words or connected by hyphens:

> To Moscow. В Москву́. *vmahsk-VOO.*
> As far as Moscow. До Москвы́. *duh-mahsk-VÏ.*
> I would like. Я хоте́л бы. *yah khah-T^yEHL-bï.*

For the convenience of the user, the accented syllables have also been marked in the Russian text of this book, though they are not normally marked in printed Russian.

CONSONANTS

Most Russian consonants have hard and soft pronunciation variants, while others are either always hard or always soft. A soft consonant is pronounced with the tongue flattened, moved slightly forward, and raised towards the roof of the mouth; this can be approximated by adding a slight *y* sound to the hard consonant. Thus the hard Russian *b* sounds like the English *b* in *booty*, while soft Russian *b*ʸ is similar to the English *b* in *beauty*. For those Russian consonants that permit both hard and soft pronunciation, the Remarks column of the chart below provides rough English equivalents for the hard variant only; the soft variant will be indicated in our transcription by a small *y* following the consonant.

Russian letter	Transcription Hard	Transcription Soft	Remarks
Б б	b	b^y	b as in *bat*.
В в	v	v^y	v as in *van*.
Г г	g	g^y	g as in *got*.
Д д	d	d^y	d as in *dog*.
Ж ж	zh	—	zh like the z in *azure*, always hard.
З з	z	z^y	z as in *zoo*.
Й й	—	y	y as in *yes* (its pronunciation in diphthongs is discussed below). y is always soft.
К к	k	k^y	k as in *sky*. In Russian, k, p and t are always pronounced without aspiration (puff of air).
Л л	l	l^y	l as in *long*.
М м	m	m^y	m as in *man*.
Н н	n	n^y	n as in *not*.
П п	p	p^y	p as in *span*.
Р р	r	r^y	r as in *ran*, but rolled with tip of tongue.
С с	s	s^y	s as in *sun*.
Т т	t	t^y	t as in *stay*.

Russian letter	Transcription Hard	Transcription Soft	Remarks
Ф ф	f	fʸ	*f* as in *fan*.
Х х	kh	khʸ	*kh* like the *ch* in German *Bach*, Scottish *loch*.
Ц ц	ts	—	*ts* as in *mats*, always hard.
Ч ч	—	ch	*ch* as in *cheese*, always soft.
Ш ш	sh	—	*sh* as in *shall*, always hard.
Щ щ	—	shh	*shh* is drawn out like the *sh* sound in *fresh sheets*; its length is indicated by the doubling of the *h* in our transcription. *shh* is always soft.

Certain combinations of consonant letters have special pronunciation as noted below.

дж	j	—	*j* as in *jam*, always hard.
сч, зч, щч, жч	—	shh	*shh* like the *sh* sound in *fresh sheets*; it is the same sound as the letter щ above.
зж, жж	—	zhh	*zhh* like the *z* in *azure*, but drawn out (indicated by doubling of *h*). *zhh* is always soft.

In consonant clusters, at the end of words, and in some other circumstances, many

Russian consonants are pronounced other than as indicated in the chart. For example, "voiced" consonants like б or д (*b*, *d*) may be pronounced without vibration of the vocal cords, that is, like *p* and *t*, respectively. The converse can also occur, so that п and т (*p*, *t*) are sometimes pronounced like *b* and *d*, respectively. Other changes include the pronunciation of г (*g*) as *v* in certain grammatical forms, and the occasional pronunciation of ч (*ch*) as *sh*. Some consonants in consonant clusters are not pronounced at all. All such modifications will be indicated in the transcription.

VOWELS

Nearly every Russian word contains one stressed syllable, that is, one syllable pronounced more loudly, with greater force, than the others (most one-syllable words in Russian are stressed). All Russian vowels are pronounced with their full value under stress but may have a different pronunciation in unstressed syllables. Russian vowel letters can be divided into two types.

Type-1 vowel letters а, э, ы, о, у indicate that a preceding consonant is hard, (except for *ch*, *shh*, *y* and *zhh*, which are always soft):

Russian letter	Transcription Stressed	Unstressed	Remarks
А а	ah	ah, uh	Under stress, at the beginning of a word, or in a syllable immediately preceding stress, *ah* like the *a*

Russian letter	Transcription		Remarks
	Stressed	Unstressed	
Э э	eh	eh	in *calm*; in other unstressed syllables *uh* like the *u* in *fun*.
			eh like the *e* in *net*.
— ы	ī	ī	No English equivalent. Something like the *i* in *bit*, but with the tongue further back and the lips spread. After *p, b, v, f,* and *m, ī* is preceded by a slight *w* sound.
О о	oh	ah, uh	Under stress, *oh* like the *o* in *more*, but short, almost like the *aw* in *awl*, pronounced with the lips rounded. It is *not* like the *o* in English *so*, which ends with an *oo* sound. At the beginning of a word or in a syllable immediately preceding stress, *ah* like the *a* in *calm*; in other unstressed syllables, *uh* like the *u* in *fun*.
У у	oo	oo	*oo* as in *loon*, but short.

Type-2 vowel letters я, е, и, ё, ю indicate that an immediately preceding consonant is soft (except for *sh*, *zh*, *ts* and *j*, which are always hard). If no consonant immediately precedes a type-2 vowel, the letter represents *y* + the corresponding vowel. Russian Ялта = *YAHL-tuh* (Yalta).

Russian letter	Transcription Stressed	Unstressed	Remarks
Я я	(y)ah	(y)ih	Under stress, *yah* like the *ya* in *yacht*; unstressed, *yih* like the *yi* in *yip*.
Е е	(y)eh	(y)ih	Under stress, *yeh* like the *ye* in *yes*; unstressed, *yih* like the *yi* in *yip*.
И и	(y)ee	(y)ee	*yee* like the *yea* in *yeast*.
Ё ё	(y)oh	—	*yoh* like the *yo* in *yore*, but short, almost like the *yaw* in *yawl*, but with lips rounded. The letter ё occurs only under stress, but the use of the dieresis " is not mandatory: Russians know from the context when to pronounce stressed е as *yeh* and when to pronounce it as *yoh*.
Ю ю	(y)oo	(y)oo	*yoo* like the *yu* in *yule*.

In certain cases, some Russian vowels are pronounced other than as indicated in these charts. For example, и is pronounced *i* after consonants that are always hard, and я and е sound like (*y*)*uh* in certain grammatical endings. All such modifications will be reflected in our transcription.

HARD AND SOFT SIGNS

Russian has two letters that have no sound value of their own; rather, they provide information about adjacent letters.

Russian letter	Transcription	Remarks
— ъ	—	The "hard sign," when it stands between a consonant and a type-2 vowel, indicates that the latter is pronounced as *y* + the corresponding vowel (объём =.*ahb-YOHM*).
— ь	*y* or —	The "soft sign" indicates that a preceding consonant is soft. If it is followed by a vowel, the vowel is pronounced as *y* + the corresponding vowel (бью = *b*ʸ*yoo*).

DIPHTHONGS

The loops under the transcription of certain Russian diphthongs indicate that they are pronounced as a single sound, in which the first element is more heavily stressed than the second. Do not pronounce the *h* as a consonant. The chart below gives the pronunciation of diphthongs in stressed syllables:

Russian letters	Transcription	Remarks
ай	ah_ee	*ah_ee* like the *ie* in *tie*.
ей	(y)eh_ee	*eh_ee* like the *ey* in *they*.
ой	oy	*oy* like the *oy* in *boy*.
уй	oo_ee	*oo_ee* like the *ooey* in *phooey*, pronounced as one syllable.
ау	ah_oo	*ah_oo* like the *ou* in *out*.
оу	o_oo	*o_oo* like the *ow* in *show*.

Some common sequences of unstressed vowel + й are as follows:

Russian letters	Transcription	Remarks
ай	ah_ee, ih_ee, uh_ee	At the beginning of a word or in a syllable immediately before stress, *ah_ee* like the *ie* in *tie*; after the consonants *ch* and *shh*, *ih_ee* like *i* (as in *it*) + *ee*; otherwise *uh_ee* like *u* (as in *fun*) + *ee*.

Russian letter	Transcription	Remarks
ой	ah_ee, uh_ee	At the beginning of a word or in a syllable immediately before stress, *ah_ee* like the *ie* in *tie*; otherwise *uh_ee* like *u* (as in *fun*) + *ee*.
ей	(y)ih_ee	*ih_ee* like *i* (as in *it*) + *ee*.
ий	ee	*ee* like *ee* in *see*.
ый	ï_ee	*ï_ee* like the *ï* described above + *ee*.

THE RUSSIAN ALPHABET

The Russian (Cyrillic) alphabet is given below with the names of the letters transcribed after them. You will need to learn the order of the letters in order to read signs, consult a Russian-English dictionary, and make the most effective use of the glossary in the back of this book; the letters' names are used in spelling out words.

Capital letter	Small letter	Transcribed name of the letter
А	а	*ah*
Б	б	*beh*
В	в	*veh*
Г	г	*geh*
Д	д	*deh*
Е	е	*yeh*
Ё	ё	*yoh*
Ж	ж	*zheh*
З	з	*zeh*
И	и	*ee*
Й	й	*ee KRAHT-kuh-yuh* (LIT.: short "ee")
К	к	*kah*
Л	л	*ehl*
М	м	*ehm*
Н	н	*ehn*
О	о	*oh*
П	п	*peh*

Capital letter	Small letter	Transcribed name of the letter
Р	р	*ehr*
С	с	*ehs*
Т	т	*teh*
У	у	*oo*
Ф	ф	*ehf*
Х	х	*khah*
Ц	ц	*tseh*
Ч	ч	*cheh*
Ш	ш	*shah*
Щ	щ	*shhah*
Ъ	ъ	*TV^{y}OHR-dï‿ee znahk* (LIT.: hard sign)
Ы	ы	*yih-RÏ*
Ь	ь	*M^{y}AHKH-k^{y}ee znahk* (LIT.: soft sign)
Э	э	*eh ah-bah-ROHT-nuh-yuh* (LIT.: backwards "eh")
Ю	ю	*yoo*
Я	я	*yah*

EVERYDAY PHRASES

1. Hello (OR: **Hi**).
Здра́вствуйте (OR: Приве́т).
ZDRAHST-voo＿ee-t^yih (OR: *pr^yee-V^yEHT*).

2. Good morning.
До́брое у́тро.　*DOH-bruh-yuh OO-truh.*

3. Good day (OR: **Good afternoon**).
До́брый де́нь.　*DOH-brï＿ee d^yehn^y.*

4. Good evening.
До́брый ве́чер.　*DOH-brï＿ee V^yEH-chihr.*

5. Good night.
Споко́йной но́чи.　*spah-KOY-nuh＿ee NOH-chee.*

6. Welcome.
Добро́ пожа́ловать.　*dah-BROH pah-ZHAH-luh-vuht^y.*

7. Goodbye.
До свида́ния.　*duh-sv^yee-DAHN^y-yuh.*

8. See you later. Пока́.　*pah-KAH.*

9. Yes. Да́.　*dah.*

10. No. Не́т.　*n^yeht.*

11. Perhaps (OR: **Maybe**).
Мо́жет бы́ть.　*MOH-zhuht bï^y.*

12. Please. Пожа́луйста.　*pah-ZHAH-lï-stuh.*

13. Allow me.
Позво́льте мне́.　*pah-ZVOHL^y-t^yih mn^yeh.*

14. Excuse me (OR: **I'm sorry**).
Извини́те (OR: Прости́те) (меня́).*
eez-v^yee-N^yEE-t^yih (OR: *prah-ST^yEE-t^yih*) (*m^yih-N^yAH*).*

---

* Меня́ (*m^yih-N^yAH*) is often omitted from both these phrases.

15. Thanks [very much].
Спасибо [большое].
spah-S^y EE-buh [bahl^y-SHOH-yuh].

16. You are welcome (OR: **Don't mention it**).
Пожалуйста (OR: Не за что).
pah-ZHAH-lï-stuh (OR: *N^y EH-zuh-shtuh*).

17. All right (OR: **Very good**).
Хорошо (OR: Очень хорошо).
khuh-rah-SHOH (OR: *OH-chihn^y khuh-rah-SHOH*).

18. It doesn't matter (OR: **It's nothing**).
Это не важно (OR: Ничего).
EH-tuh n^y ih-VAHZH-nuh (OR: *n^y ee-chih-VOH*).

19. Don't bother.
Не беспокойтесь. *n^y ih-b^y ih-spah-KOY-t^y ihs^y.*

20. You have been very kind.
Вы были очень добры.
vï BÏ-l^y ee OH-chihn^y dah-BRÏ.

21. You have been very helpful.
Вы очень помогли. *vï OH-chihn^y puh-mah-GL^y EE.*

22. Come in. Заходите. *zuh-khah-D^y EE-t^y ih.*

23. Come here.
Подойдите сюда.
puh-dah_ee-D^y EE-t^y ih s^y oo-DAH.

24. Come with me.
Пойдёмте со мной. *pah_ee-D^y OHM-t^y ih sahm-NOY.*

25. Come back later.
Вернитесь позже. *v^y ihr-N^y EE-t^y ihs^y POH-zhhih.*

26. Come early.
Приходите пораньше.
pr^y ee-khah-D^y EE-t^y ih pah-RAHN^y-shï.

27. Wait a minute. Минутку. *m^y ee-NOOT-koo.*

28. Wait for us.
Подождите нас.   *puh-dahzh-D^yEE-t^yih nahs.*

29. Not yet.   Нет ещё.   *n^yeht yih-SHHOH.*

30. Right away.   Сейчас.   *s^yih-CHAHS.*

31. Not now.   Не сейчас.   *n^yih-s^yih-CHAHS.*

32. Listen.   Послушайте.   *pah-SLOO-shuh_ee-t^yih.*

33. Look out!   Осторожно!   *ah-stah-ROHZH-nuh!*

34. Be careful.
Будьте осторожны.   *BOOT^y-t^yih ah-stah-ROHZH-nï.*

SOCIAL PHRASES

35. May I introduce [Mrs. Elena Nikolaevna Petrov]?*
Разрешите представить [Елену Николаевну Петрову].
*ruhz-r^yih-SHĬ-t^yih pr^yiht-STAH-v^yeet^y [yih-L^yEH-noo
n^yee-kah-LAH-yihv-noo p^yih-TROH-voo].*

36. —Mr. Alexei Vladimirovich Petrov.*
—Алексея Владимировича Петрова.
*—ah-l^yihk-S^yEH-yuh vlah-D^yEE-m^yee-ruh-v^yee-chuh
p^yih-TROH-vuh.*

* The most appropriate way of addressing Russians is by their
first name and patronymic (derived from their father's name).
Thus, Elena Nikolaevna Petrov would normally be addressed as
Elena Nikolaevna, without any title. In very formal situations, the
title товарищ (*tah-VAH-r^yeeshh*, "comrade") may be used
together with the last name. As a foreigner, you will often be
addressed with the titles господин (*guh-spah-D^yEEN*) for men,
and госпожа (*guh-spah-ZHAH*) for women, together with your
last name.

37. Pleased to meet you.

Очень прия́тно (познако́миться с ва́ми).

OH-chihn^y pr^yee-YAHT-nuh (puh-znah-KOH-m^yeet-tsuh SVAH-m^yee).

38. How are you?

Как поживаете? *kahk puh-zhï-VAH-yih-t^yih?*

39. Very well, thanks, and you?

Спаси́бо, хорошо́, а вы́?

spah-S^yEE-buh, khuh-rah-SHOH, ah-VÏ?

40. How are things? Как дела́? *kahk d^yih-LAH?*

41. All right (OR: **Fine**).

Хорошо́ (OR: Ничего́).

khuh-rah-SHOH (OR: *n^yee-chih-VOH*).

42. So, so. Та́к себе́. *tahk s^yih-B^yEH.*

43. What's new? Что́ но́вого? *shtoh NOH-vuh-vuh?*

44. Please have a seat.

Сади́тесь, пожа́луйста.

sah-D^yEE-t^yihs^y, pah-ZHAH-lï-stuh.

45. It's a pleasure to see you again.

Очень прия́тно ва́с ви́деть опя́ть.

OH-chihn^y pr^yee-YAHT-nuh vahs V^yEE-d^yiht^y ah-P^yAHT^y.

46. Congratulations (LIT.: **I/we congratulate**).

Поздравля́ю/Поздравля́ем.

puh-zdrahv-L^yAH-yoo/puh-zdrahv-L^yAH-yihm.

47. All the best.

Всего́ наилу́чшего.

fs^yih-VOH nuh-ee-LOOCH-shuh-vuh.

48. I like you very much.

Вы́ мне́ о́чень нра́витесь.

vï mn^yeh OH-chihn^y NRAH-v^yee-t^yihs^y.

49. I love you. Я люблю вác. *yah lʸoo-BLʸOO vahs.*

50. May I see you again?
Мóжно вáс увúдеть ещё рáз?
MOHZH-nuh vahs oo-VʸEE-dʸihtʸ yih-SHHOH rahs?

51. Let's make a date for next week.
Назнáчим свидáние на бýдущей недéле.
nah-ZNAH-chihm svʸee-DAH-nʸee-yuh nah-BOO-doo-shhih＿ee nʸih-DʸEH-lʸih.

52. I have enjoyed myself very much.
Мнé бы́ло óчень прия́тно.
mnʸeh BĬ-luh OH-chihnʸ prʸee-YAHT-nuh.

53. Give my regards [to your friend].
Передáйте привéт [вáшему прия́телю (F.: вáшей
прия́тельнице)].
pʸih-rʸih-DAH＿EE-tʸih prʸee-VʸEHT [VAH-shuh-moo prʸee-YAH-tʸih-lʸoo (F.: VAH-shuh＿ee prʸee-YAH-tʸilʸ-nʸee-tsĭ)].

54. —your girlfriend.
—вáшей подрýге. —*VAH-shuh＿ee pah-DROO-gʸih.*

55. —your boyfriend.
—вáшему молодóму человéку.
—*VAH-shuh-moo muh-lah-DOH-moo chih-lah-VʸEH-koo.*

See also "Family," p. 170.

BASIC QUESTIONS

56. What? Чтó? *shtoh?*

57. What did you say?
Чтó вы́ сказáли? *shtoh vĭ skah-ZAH-lʸee?*

58. What is that?
Чтó тáм такóе? *shtoh tahm tah-KOH-yuh?*

59. What is this?
Что́ э́то тако́е? *shtoh EH-tuh tah-KOH-yuh?*

60. What must I do?
Что́ я до́лжен (F.: должна́) де́лать?
shtoh yah DOHL-zhuhn (F.: dahlzh-NAH) D^yEH-luht^y?

61. What is the matter?
В чём де́ло? *fchohm D^yEH-luh?*

62. What do you want?
Что́ вы хоти́те? *shtoh vï khah-T^yEE-t^yih?*

63. When? Когда́? *kahg-DAH?*

64. When does it [leave]?
Когда́ он [отхо́дит]?
kahg-DAH ohn [aht-KHOH-d^yiht]?

65. —arrive. —прихо́дит. *—pr^yee-KHOH-d^yiht.*

66. —begin. —начина́ется. *—nuh-chee-NAH-yiht-tsuh.*

67. —end. —конча́ется. *—kahn-CHAH-yiht-tsuh.*

68. Where? Где́? *gd^yeh?*

69. Whither (to what place)? Куда́? *koo-DAH?*

70. Whence (from what place)?
Отку́да? *aht-KOO-duh?*

71. Where is it?
Где́ он (F.: она́, N.: оно́)?
gd^yeh ohn (F.: ah-NAH, N.: ah-NOH)?

72. Where is the bathroom (OR: restroom)?
Где́ туале́т? *gd^yeh too-ah-L^yEHT?*

73. Why? Почему́? *puh-chih-MOO?*

74. How? Ка́к? *kahk?*

75. How long? Ка́к до́лго? *kahk DOHL-guh?*

76. How far? Ка́к далеко́? *kahk duh-l^yih-KOH?*

77. How much? (OR: **How many?**)
Ско́лько? *SKOHL^y-kuh?*

78. How do you do it?
Ка́к вы э́то де́лаете?
kahk vï EH-tuh D^yEH-luh-yih-t^yih?

79. How does it work?
Ка́к э́то рабо́тает?
kahk EH-tuh rah-BOH-tuh-yiht?

80. Who? Кто́? *ktoh?*

81. Who are you? Кто́ вы? *ktoh vï?*

82. Who is [that boy]?
Кто́ [э́тот ма́льчик]? *ktoh [EH-tuht MAHL^y-cheek]?*

83. —that young man.
—э́тот молодо́й челове́к.
—EH-tuht muh-lah-DOY chih-lah-V^yEHK.

84. —that girl.
—э́та де́вушка. *—EH-tuh D^yEH-voosh-kuh.*

85. —that man.
—э́тот мужчи́на. *—EH-tuht moo-SHHEE-nuh.*

86. —that woman.
—э́та же́нщина. *—EH-tuh ZHEHN-shhee-nuh.*

87. Am I [on time]?
Я пришёл (F.: пришла́) [во́-время]?
yah pr^yee-SHOHL (F.: pr^yee-SHLAH) [VOH-vr^yih-m^yuh]?

88. —early. —ра́но. *—RAH-nuh.*

89. —late. —по́здно. *—POHZ-nuh.*

TALKING ABOUT YOURSELF

90. What is your name?

Ка́к ва́с зову́т? *kahk vahs zah-VOOT?*

91. My name is [Boris Mikhailovich Sverdlov] [Tatiana Vasilievna Zhukov].

Меня́ зову́т [Бори́с Миха́йлович Свердло́в] [Татья́на Васи́льевна Жу́кова].

m'ih-N'AH zah-VOOT [bah-R'EES m'ee-KHAH＿EE-luh-v'eech sv'ihrd-LOHF] [taht'-YAH-nuh vah-S'EEL'-yihv-nuh ZHOO-kuh-vuh].

92. My name is [Ivan].

Моё и́мя — [Ива́н].

mah-YOH EE-m'uh — [ee-VAHN].

93. I am [21 years old].

Мне́ [два́дцать оди́н го́д].

mn'eh [DVAHT-tsuht' ah-D'EEN goht].

94. —34 years old.

—три́дцать четы́ре го́да.

—TR'EET-tsuht' chih-TÏ-r'ih GOH-duh.

95. —47 years old.

—со́рок се́мь ле́т.   *—SOH-ruhk s'ehm' l'eht.*

96. I am [an American citizen].

Я́ — [америка́нский граждани́н (ғ.: америка́нская гражда́нка)].

yah — [ah-m'ih-r'ee-KAHN-sk'ee gruzh-dah-N'EEN (ғ.: ah-m'ih-r'ee-KAHN-skuh-yuh grahzh-DAHN-kuh)].

97. My address is [National Hotel, Marx Prospect 14, Room 223, Moscow].

Мо́й а́дрес—[Гости́ница «Национа́ль», Проспе́кт Ма́ркса 14, Но́мер 223, Москва́].

moy AH-dr'ihs — [gah-ST'EE-n'ee-tsuh "nuh-tsï-ah-

NAHL^y'', *prah-SP^yEHKT MAHRK-suh chih-TÏR-
nuht-tsuht^y, NOH-m^yihr DV^yEH-st^yee DVAHT-tsuht^y
tr^yee, mahsk-VAH*].

98. I am [a high school student].
Я — [учени́к (F.: учени́ца)].
yah — [oo-chih-N^yEEK (F.: oo-chih-N^yEE-tsuh)].

99. —a college student.
—студе́нт (F.: студе́нтка).
—stoo-D^yEHNT (F.: stoo-D^yEHNT-kuh).

100. —a high school teacher.
—учи́тель (F.: учи́тельница).
—oo-CHEE-t^yihl^y (F.: oo-CHEE-t^yihl^y-n^yee-tsuh).

101. I teach [in a college] [in a university].
Я преподаю́ [в колле́дже] [в университе́те].
*yah pr^yih-puh-dah-YOO [fkah-L^yEH-ji] [voo-n^yee-v^yihr-
s^yee-T^yEH-t^yih].*

102. I am [a businessman].
Я — [бизнесме́н]. *yah — [b^yeez-nehs-MEHN].*

103. What is your job? (OR: What is your profession?)
Кака́я у ва́с рабо́та? (OR: Кто́ вы́ по профе́ссии?)
*kah-KAH-yuh oo-VAHS rah-BOH-tuh? (OR: ktoh vï
puh-prah-F^yEH-s^yee-yee?)*

104. I am a friend of [Ivan Sergeyevich Ivanov].
Я прия́тель (F.: прия́тельница) [Ива́на Серге́евича
Ива́нова].
*yah pr^yee-YAH-t^yihl^y (F.: pr^yee-YAH-t^yihl^y-n^yee-tsuh)
[ee-VAH-nuh s^yihr-G^yEH-yih-v^yee-chuh
ee-VAH-nuh-vuh].*

105. He works [for the Nauka Publishing House].
Он рабо́тает [в изда́тельстве «Нау́ка»].
*ohn rah-BOH-tuh-yiht [vïz-DAH-t^yihl^y-stv^yih
"nah-OO-kuh"].*

106. I am here [on vacation].
Я здесь [в о́тпуске].
yah zdᵞehsᵞ [VOHT-poo-skᵞih].

107. —on a business trip.
—в командиро́вке.   *—fkuh-muhn-dᵞee-ROHF-kᵞih.*

108. I have been here [one week].
Я здесь уже́ [одну́ неде́лю].
yah zdᵞehsᵞ oo-ZHEH [ahd-NOO nᵞih-DᵞEH-lᵞoo].

109. We plan to stay here until [Friday].
Мы собира́емся оста́ться здесь до [пя́тницы].
mï suh-bᵞee-RAH-yihm-suh ah-STAHT-tsuh zdᵞehsᵞ
   dah-[Pᵞ AHT-nᵞee-tsï].

110. I am traveling to [Moscow].
Я е́ду в [Москву́].   *yah YEH-doo v[mahsk-VOO].*

111. I am in a hurry.
Я спешу́.   *yah spᵞih-SHOO.*

112. I am [cold].
Мне [хо́лодно].   *mnᵞeh [KHOH-luhd-nuh].*

113. —warm.   —тепло́.   *—tᵞih-PLOH.*

114. —thirsty.
—хо́чется пи́ть.   *—KHOH-chiht-tsuh pᵞeetᵞ.*

115. I am [busy].
Я [за́нят (F.: занята́)].
yah [ZAH-nᵞiht (F.: zuh-nᵞih-TAH)].

116. —tired.   —уста́л (F.: уста́ла).   *—oo-STAHL (F.: oo-STAH-luh).*

117. —hungry.
—го́лоден (F.: голодна́).
—GOH-luh-dᵞihn (F.: guh-lahd-NAH).

118. —glad.   —ра́д (F.: ра́да).   *—raht (F.: RAH-duh).*

119. —disappointed.
—разочаро́ван (F.: разочаро́вана).
—*ruh-zuh-chih-ROH-vuhn* (F.: *ruh-zuh-chih-ROH-vuh-nuh*).

120. I cannot do it.
Я не могу́ сде́лать э́то.
yah nʸih-mah-GOO ZDʸEH-luhtʸ EH-tuh.

121. We are [happy].
Мы [сча́стливы].   *mï [SHHAHS-lʸee-vï].*

122. —unhappy.
—несча́стны.   —*nʸih-SHHAHS-nï.*

123. —angry.   —серди́ты.   —*sʸihr-DʸEE-tï.*

MAKING YOURSELF UNDERSTOOD

124. Do you speak [English]?
Вы говори́те [по-англи́йски]?
vï guh-vah-RʸEE-tʸih [pah-ahn-GLʸEE-skʸee]?

125. Where is [English] spoken?
Где говоря́т [по-англи́йски]?
gdʸeh guh-vah-RʸAHT [pah-ahn-GLʸEE-skʸee]?

126. Does anyone here speak [French]?
Кто́-нибудь зде́сь говори́т [по-францу́зски]?
KTOH-nʸee-bootʸ zdʸehsʸ guh-vah-RʸEET [puh-frahn-TSOO-skʸee]?

127. I read only [Italian].
Я чита́ю то́лько [по-италья́нски].
yah chee-TAH-yoo TOHLʸ-kuh [puh-ee-tahlʸ-YAHN-skʸee].

128. I speak a little [German].
Я немно́го говорю́ [по-неме́цки].
yah n'ihm-NOH-guh guh-vah-R'OO [puh-n'ih-M'EHTS-k'ee].

129. Speak more slowly.
Говори́те ме́дленнее.
guh-vah-R'EE-t'ih M'EH-dl'ihn-n'ih-yih.

130. I [do not] understand.
Я [не] понима́ю. *yah [n'ih]-puh-n'ee-MAH-yoo.*

131. Do you understand me?
Вы понима́ете меня́?
vï puh-n'ee-MAH-yih-t'ih m'ih-N'AH?

132. I [do not] know.
Я [не] зна́ю. *yah [n'ih]-ZNAH-yoo.*

133. I think so.
Я ду́маю, что да́. *yah DOO-muh-yoo, shtuh-DAH.*

134. I don't think so.
Я ду́маю, что нет. *yah DOO-muh-yoo, shtuh-N'EHT.*

135. Repeat it. Повтори́те. *puhf-tah-R'EE-t'ih.*

136. Write it down.
Запиши́те. *zuh-p'ee-SHÏ-t'ih.*

137. Answer "yes" or "no."
Отве́тьте «да» и́ли «нет».
aht-V'EHT'-t'ih "dah" EE-l'ee "n'eht".

138. You are right. Вы пра́вы. *vï PRAH-vï.*

139. You are wrong.
Вы не пра́вы. *vï n'ih-PRAH-vï.*

140. What does [this word] mean?
Что зна́чит [э́то сло́во]?
shtoh ZNAH-chiht [EH-tuh SLOH-vuh]?

141. How do you say ["pencil"] in Russian?
Как сказа́ть по-ру́сски ["pencil"]?
kahk skah-ZAHT[y] pah-ROO-sk[y]ee ["pencil"]?

142. How do you spell [Vladivostok]?
Как пи́шется [Владивосто́к]?
kahk P[y]EE-shuht-tsuh [vluh-d[y]ee-vah-STOHK]?

DIFFICULTIES AND
MISUNDERSTANDINGS

143. Where is [the American Embassy]?
Где [америка́нское посо́льство]?
gd[y]eh [ah-m[y]ih-r[y]ee-KAHN-skuh-yuh pah-SOHL[y]-stvuh]?

144. —the American consulate.
—америка́нское ко́нсульство.
—ah-m[y]ih-r[y]ih-KAHN-skuh-yuh KOHN-sool[y]-stvuh.

145. —the police station.
—отделе́ние мили́ции.
—ahd-d[y]ih-L[y]EH-n[y]ee-yuh m[y]ee-L[y]EE-tsï-yee.

146. —the lost-and-found office.
—бюро́ нахо́док.
—b[y]oo-ROH nah-KHOH-duhk.

147. I want to talk [to the manager].
Я хочу́ поговори́ть [с заве́дующим].
yah khah-CHOO puh-guh-vah-R[y]EET[y] [zzah-V[y]EH-doo-yoo-shhihm].

148. —your superior.
—с ва́шим нача́льником.
—SVAH-shïm nah-CHAHL[y]-n[y]ee-kuhm.

149. Bring me the complaint book.*

Принесите книгу жалоб.

pr^yee-n^yih-S^yEE-t^yih KN^yEE-goo ZHAH-luhp.

150. Can you help me?

Вы сможете мне помочь?

vï SMOH-zhuh-t^yih mn^yeh pah-MOHCH?

151. Can you tell me how to get there (driving/walking)?

Скажите (мне), как проехать/пройти туда.

skah-ZHÏ-t^yih (mn^yeh), kahk prah-YEH-khuht^y/prah‿ee-T^yEE too-DAH.

152. I am looking for my friend.

Я ищу своего приятеля (F.: свою приятельницу).

yah ee-SHHOO svuh-yih-VOH pr^yee-YAH-t^yih-l^yuh (F.: svah-YOO pr^yee-YAH-t^yihl^y-n^yee-tsoo).

153. I am lost.

Я заблудился (F.: заблудилась).

yah zuh-bloo-D^yEEL-suh (F.: zuh-bloo-D^yEE-luhs^y).

154. I cannot find [the address].

Я не могу найти [адрес].

yah n^yih-mah-GOO nah‿ee-T^yEE [AH-dr^yihs].

155. She has lost [her handbag].

Она потеряла [свою сумку].

ah-NAH puh-t^yih-R^yAH-luh [svah-YOO SOOM-koo].

156. He has lost [his wallet].

Он потерял [свой бумажник].

ohn puh-t^yih-R^yAHL [svoy boo-MAHZH-n^yeek].

---

* Every Soviet establishment has a complaint book in which customers can register complaints about poor service, surliness, rudeness, etc. Such complaints are taken quite seriously by superiors.

157. We forgot [our keys].
Мы забыли [(наши) ключи́].
mï zah-BÏ-lʸee [(NAH-shï) klʸoo-CHEE].

158. We missed [the train].
Мы опозда́ли на [по́езд].
mï ah-pah-ZDAH-lʸee nah-[POH-yihst].

159. It is not my fault.
Э́то не моя́ вина́. *EH-tuh nʸih-mah-YAH vʸee-NAH.*

160. I do not remember [the first name] [the surname].
Я не по́мню [и́мя] [фами́лию].
yah nʸih-POHM-nʸoo [EE-mʸuh] [fah-MʸEE-lʸee-yoo].

161. What is wrong?
Что случи́лось? *shtoh sloo-CHEE-luhsʸ?*

162. What shall I do?
Что мне де́лать? *shtoh mnʸeh DʸEH-luhtʸ?*

163. Leave us alone!
Оста́вьте нас в поко́е!
ah-STAHFʸ-tʸih nahs fpah-KOH-yih!

164. Go away! (OR: **Scram!**)
Уйди́те! (OR: Убира́йтесь!)
oo＿ee-DʸEE-tʸih! (OR: *oo-bʸee-RAH＿EE-tʸihsʸ!*)

165. Help! Помоги́те! *puh-mah-GʸEE-tʸih!*

166. Police! Мили́ция! *mʸee-LʸEE-tsï-yuh!*

167. Thief! Вор! *vohr!*

168. Fire! Пожа́р! *pah-ZHAHR!*

169. Look out! Осторо́жно! *ah-stah-ROHZH-nuh!*

170. This is an emergency.
Э́то э́кстренный слу́чай.
EH-tuh EHK-strʸihn-nï＿ee SLOO-chih＿ee.

CUSTOMS

171. Where is [the customs office]?
Где [таможня]?   *gd^yeh [tah-MOHZH-n^yuh]?*

172. Here is [our baggage].
Вот [наш багаж].   *voht [nahsh bah-GAHSH].*

173. —my passport.
—мой паспорт.   *—moy PAHS-puhrt.*

174. —my identification card.
—моё удостоверение личности.
—mah-YOH oo-duh-stuh-v^yih-R^yEH-n^yee-yuh L^yEECH-nuh-st^yee.

175. —my health certificate.
—моя справка о здоровье.
—mah-YAH SPRAHF-kuh ah-zdah-ROHV^y-yih.

176. —my [visitor's] visa.
—моя [гостевая] виза.
—mah-YAH [guh-st^yih-VAH-yuh] V^yEE-zuh.

177. I am in transit.
Я здесь по транзитной визе.
yah zd^yehs^y puh-trahn-Z^yEET-nuh＿ee V^yEE-z^yih.

178. [The bags] over there are mine.
[Чемоданы] там — мой.
[chih-mah-DAH-nï] tahm — mah-YEE.

179. Must I open everything?
Должен (F.: должна) ли я всё открыть?
DOHL-zhuhn (F.: dahlzh-NAH)-l^yee yah fs^yoh aht-KRÏT^y?

180. I cannot open [the trunk].
Я не могу открыть [сундук].
yah n^yih-mah-GOO aht-KRÏT^y [soon-DOOK].

181. There is nothing here [but clothing].
Здесь нет ничего [кроме одежды].
*zd^yehs^y n^yeht n^yee-chih-VOH [KROH-m^yih
ah-D^yEHZH-dï].*

182. I have nothing to declare (LIT.: I have no valuables).
У меня нет никаких ценностей.
*oo-m^yih-N^yAH n^yeht n^yee-kah-K^yEEKH TSEHN-nuh-
st^yih_ee.*

183. Everything is for my personal use.
Всё для личного пользования.
fs^yoh dl^yah-L^yEECH-nuh-vuh POHL^y-zuh-vuh-n^yee-yuh.

184. I bought [this necklace] in the United States.
Я купил (F.: купила) [это ожерелье] в Соединённых
Штатах.
*yah koo-P^yEEL (F.: koo-P^yEE-luh) [EH-tuh ah-zhï-
R^yEHL^y-yuh] fsuh-yih-d^yee-N^yOHN-nïkh
SHTAH-tuhkh.*

185. These are [gifts]. Это — [подарки]. *EH-tuh — [pah-DAHR-k^yee].*

186. This is all I have.
Это всё, что у меня есть.
EH-tuh FS^yOH-shtuh oo-m^yih-N^yAH yehst^y.

187. Must duty be paid on [these things]?
Облагаются ли [эти вещи] пошлиной?
*ahb-lah-GAH-yoot-tsuh-l^yee [EH-t^yee V^yEH-shhee]
POHSH-l^yee-nuh_ee?*

188. Have you finished the inspection?
Вы окончили досмотр?
vï ah-KOHN-chee-l^yee dah-SMOH-tuhr?

BAGGAGE

189. Where can we check our luggage through to [Moscow]?

Где мо́жно сда́ть наш бага́ж до [Москвы́]?

gdᵞeh MOHZH-nuh zdahtᵞ nahsh bah-GAHSH duh-[mahsk-VÏ]?

190. These things to the [left] [right] belong to me.

Э́ти ве́щи [сле́ва] [спра́ва]—мой.

EH-tᵞee VᵞEH-shhee [SLᵞEH-vuh] [SPRAH-vuh] — mah-YEE.

191. I cannot find all my baggage.

Я не могу́ найти́ весь мой бага́ж.

yah nᵞih-mah-GOO nah‿ee-TᵞEE vᵞehsᵞ moy bah-GAHSH.

192. I am missing [one suitcase].

У меня́ не хвата́ет [одного́ чемода́на].

oo-mᵞih-NᵞAH nᵞih-khvah-TAH-yiht [ahd-nah-VOH chih-mah-DAH-nuh].

193. I want to leave [this suitcase] here [for a few days].

Я хочу́ оста́вить [э́тот чемода́н] здесь [на не́сколько дней].

yah khah-CHOO ah-STAH-vᵞeetᵞ [EH-tuht chih-mah-DAHN] zdᵞehsᵞ [nah-NᵞEH-skuhlᵞ-kuh dnᵞeh‿ee].

194. Give me a receipt for the baggage.

Да́йте мне квита́нцию на бага́ж.

DAH‿EE-tᵞih mnᵞeh kvᵞee-TAHN-tsï-yoo nuh-bah-GAHSH.

195. I have [a black trunk].

У меня́ есть [чёрный сунду́к].

oo-mᵞih-NᵞAH yehstᵞ [CHOHR-nï‿ee soon-DOOK].

196. —four pieces of luggage altogether.

—всего́ четы́ре ме́ста багажа́.

—*fsᵞih-VOH chih-TЇ-rᵞih MᵞEH-stuh buh-gah-ZHAH.*

197. Carry this suitcase to the baggage room.

Отнеси́те э́тот чемода́н в ка́меру хране́ния.

aht-nᵞih-SᵞEE-tᵞih EH-tuht chih-mah-DAHN
  FKAH-mᵞih-roo khrah-NᵞEH-nᵞee-yuh.

198. Don't forget that.

Не забу́дьте э́то. *nᵞih-zah-BOOTᵞ-tᵞih EH-tuh.*

199. I shall carry this myself.

Я понесу́ э́то са́м (F.: сама́).

yah puh-nᵞih-SOO EH-tuh sahm (F.: sah-MAH).

200. Follow me.

Иди́те за мно́й. *ee-DᵞEE-tᵞih zahm-NOY.*

201. I need a porter.

Мне́ ну́жен носи́льщик.

mnᵞeh NOO-zhuhn nah-SᵞEELᵞ-shheek.

202. This is very [fragile].

Э́то о́чень [хру́пкая ве́щь].

EH-tuh OH-chihnᵞ [KHROOP-kuh-yuh vᵞehshh].

203. Handle this carefully.

Осторо́жно, пожа́луйста.

ah-stah-ROHZH-nuh, pah-ZHAH-lï-stuh.

204. How much do I owe you?

Ско́лько я́ ва́м до́лжен (F.: должна́)?

SKOHLᵞ-kuh yah vahm DOHL-zhuhn (F.: dahlzh-NAH)?

205. What is the customary tip? (LIT.: How much is usually given for tea?)

Ско́лько обы́чно даю́т на ча́й?

SKOHLᵞ-kuh ah-BЇCH-nuh dah-YOOT nah-CHAH＿EE?

TRAVEL DIRECTIONS

206. I want to go [to the airline office].
Я хочу́ пое́хать [в авиака́ссу].
yah khah-CHOO pah-YEH-khuht [*VAH-v*ʸ*ee-ah-KAHS-soo*].

207. —to the travel agent's office.
—в бюро́ путеше́ствий.
*—vb*ʸ*oo-ROH poo-t*ʸ*ih-SHEH-stv*ʸ*ee.*

208. —to Intourist (government tourist office).
—в бюро́ Интури́ста.
*—vb*ʸ*oo-ROH een-too-R*ʸ*EE-stuh.*

209. How long does it take to walk [to Red Square]?
Ка́к до́лго идти́ [до Кра́сной пло́щади]?
*kahk DOHL-guh eet-T*ʸ*EE* [*dah-KRAHS-nuh ͜ ee PLOH-shhih-d*ʸ*ee*]?

210. Is this the shortest way [to the Kremlin]?
Э́то са́мый коро́ткий пу́ть [к Кремлю́]?
*EH-tuh SAH-m*ï ͜ *ee kah-ROHT-k*ʸ*ee poot*ʸ
[*kkr*ʸ*ihm-L*ʸ*OO*]?

211. How does one get [to the center of town]?
Ка́к попа́сть [в центр го́рода]?
*kahk pah-PAHST*ʸ [*FTSEHN-tuhr GOH-ruh-duh*]?

212. —to a department store.
—в универма́г. —*voo-n*ʸ*ee-v*ʸ*ihr-MAHK.*

213. Do I turn [to the north] [to the south] [to the east] [to the west]?
Поверну́ть [на се́вер] [на юг] [на восто́к] [на за́пад]?
*puh-v*ʸ*ihr-NOOT*ʸ [*nah-S*ʸ*EH-v*ʸ*ihr*] [*nah-YOOK*]
[*nuh-vah-STOHK*] [*nah-ZAH-puht*]?

214. What street is this?

Кака́я э́то у́лица?

kah-KAH-yuh EH-tuh OO-l^{y}ee-tsuh?

215. How far is it from here?

Ка́к далеко́ отсю́да?

kahk duh-l^{y}ih-KOH aht-S^{y}OO-duh?

216. Is it near or far?

Бли́зко и́ли далеко́?

BL^{y}EES-kuh EE-l^{y}ee duh-l^{y}ih-KOH?

217. Can we walk there?

Мо́жно туда́ пешко́м?

MOHZH-nuh too-DAH p^{y}ihsh-KOHM?

218. Am I going (walking/riding) in the right direction?

Я иду́/е́ду в пра́вильном направле́нии?

yah ee-DOO/YEH-doo FPRAH-v^{y}eel^y-nuhm nuh-prahv-L^{y}EH-n^{y}ee-yee?

219. Please point.

Покажи́те, пожа́луйста.

puh-kah-ZHĬ-t^{y}ih, pah-ZHAH-lĭ-stuh.

220. Should I go [this way] [that way]?

Мне́ идти́ [сюда́] [туда́]?

mn^{y}eh eet-T^{y}EE [s^{y}oo-DAH] [too-DAH]?

221. Turn [right] [left] at the next corner.

Поверни́те [напра́во] [нале́во] на сле́дующем углу́.

puh-v^{y}ihr-N^{y}EE-t^{y}ih [nah-PRAH-vuh] [nah-L^{y}EH-vuh] nah-SL^{y}EH-doo-yoo-shhihm oo-GLOO.

222. Is it [on this side of the street]?

Э́то [на э́той стороне́ у́лицы]?

EH-tuh [nah-EH-tuh͜ee stuh-rah-N^{y}EH OO-l^{y}ee-tsĭ]?

223.   —on the other side of the street.
—на другóй сторонé ýлицы.
*—nuh-droo-GOY stuh-rah-N*ʸ*EH OO-l*ʸ*ee-tsï.*

224.   —across the bridge.
—чéрез мóст.   *—chih-r*ʸ*ihz-MOHST.*

225.   —along the boulevard.
—по бульвáру.   *—puh-bool*ʸ*-VAH-roo.*

226.   —between these avenues.
—мéжду э́тими проспéктами.
*—M*ʸ*EHZH-doo EH-t*ʸ*ee-m*ʸ*ee prah-SP*ʸ*EHK-tuh-m*ʸ*ee.*

227.   —beyond the traffic light.
—за светофóром.   *—zuh-sv*ʸ*ih-tah-FOH-ruhm.*

228.   —next to the apartment house.
—ря́дом с жилы́м дóмом.
*—R*ʸ*AH-duhm zhzhï-LÏM DOH-muhm.*

229.   —in the middle of the block.
—в середи́не квартáла.
*—fs*ʸ*ih-r*ʸ*ih-D*ʸ*EE-n*ʸ*ih kvahr-TAH-luh.*

230.   —straight ahead.   —пря́мо.   *—PR*ʸ*AH-muh.*

231.   —near the embankment.
—óколо нáбережной.
*—OH-kuh-luh NAH-b*ʸ*ih-r*ʸ*ihzh-nuh␣ee.*

232.   —inside the station.
—внутри́ вокзáла.   *—vnoo-TR*ʸ*EE vahg-ZAH-luh.*

233.   —near the square.
—óколо плóщади.
*—OH-kuh-luh PLOH-shhih-d*ʸ*ee.*

234.   —outside the lobby (hotel/theater).
—у вхóда в вестибю́ль/в фойé.
*—oof-KHOH-duh vv*ʸ*ih-st*ʸ*ee-B*ʸ*OOL*ʸ*/ffah-YEH.*

235. —at the entrance.
—у вхо́да.   *—oof-KHOH-duh.*

236. —opposite the park.
—напро́тив па́рка.   *—nah-PROH-t^yeef PAHR-kuh.*

237. —beside the school.
—ря́дом со шко́лой.
—R^YAH-duhm sah-SHKOH-luh ‿ee.

238. —in front of the monument.
—пе́ред па́мятником.
—P^yEH-r^yiht PAH-m^yiht-n^yee-kuhm.

239. —in the rear of the store.
—позади́ магази́на.
—puh-zah-D^yEE muh-gah-Z^yEE-nuh.

240. —behind the building.
—за зда́нием.   *—zah-ZDAH-n^yee-yihm.*

241. —up the hill.   —на горе́.   *—nuh-gah-R^yEH.*

242. —down the stairs.
—внизу́.   *—vn^yee-ZOO.*

243. —at the top of the escalator.
—наверху́ эскала́тора.
—nuh-v^yihr-KHOO eh-skah-LAH-tuh-ruh.

244. —around the traffic circle.
—по кольцево́й развя́зке.
—puh-kuhl^y-tsï-VOY rahz-V^yAHS-k^yih.

245. The factory (heavy industry/light industry).
Заво́д/Фа́брика.   *zah-VOHT/FAH-br^yee-kuh.*

246. The office building.
Администрати́вное зда́ние.
ahd-m^yee-n^yee-strah-T^yEEV-nuh-yuh ZDAH-n^yee-yuh.

247. The residential section.
Жило́й райо́н.   *zhï-LOY rah-YOHN.*

24 BOAT

248. The suburbs.
Пригороды. *PR^{y}EE-guh-ruh-dï.*
249. The city. Город. *GOH-ruht.*
250. The country.
Дере́вня. *d^{y}ih-R^{y}EHV-n^{y}uh.*
251. The village.
Село́ (OR: Дере́вня).
s^{y}ih-LOH (OR: *d^{y}ih-R^{y}EHV-n^{y}uh*).

BOAT

252. When must I go on board?
Когда́ я до́лжен (F.: должна́) сесть на теплохо́д?
kahg-DAH yah DOHL-zhuhn (F.: *dahl-ZHNAH*) *s^{y}ehst^y nuh-t^{y}ih-plah-KHOHT?*

253. Bon voyage!
Счастли́вого пути́!
shhihs-L^{y}EE-vuh-vuh poo-T^{y}EE!

254. I want to rent a deck chair.
Я хочу́ взять шезло́нг на прока́т.
yah khah-CHOO vz^{y}aht^y shehz-LOHNK nuh-prah-KAHT.

255. Can we go ashore [at Odessa]?
Мо́жно вы́садиться [в Оде́ссе]?
MOHZH-nuh VÏ-suh-d^{y}eet-tsuh [vah-D^{y}EH-s^{y}ih]?

256. At what time is dinner served?
В кото́ром часу́ подаю́т обе́д?
fkah-TOH-ruhm chih-SOO puh-dah-YOOT ah-B^{y}EHT?

257. When is [the first sitting] [the second sitting]?
Когда́ обе́дает [пе́рвая сме́на] [втора́я сме́на]?

kahg-DAH ah-B^yEH-duh-yiht [*P^yEHR-vuh-yuh*
SM^yEH-nuh] [*ftah-RAH-yuh SM^yEH-nuh*]?

258. I feel (sea)sick.

Меня тошнит.   *m^yih-N^yAH tahsh-N^yEET.*

259. Have you a remedy for seasickness?

У вас есть средство от морской болезни?
oo-VAHS yehst^y SR^yEHT-stvuh aht-mahr-SKOY
bah-L^yEHZ-n^yee?

260. Lifeboat.

Спасательная лодка.
spah-SAH-t^yihl^y-nuh-yuh LOHT-kuh.

261. Life preserver.

Спасательный пояс.
spah-SAH-t^yihl^y-nï͜ee POH-yihs.

262. The ferry. Паром.   *pah-ROHM.*

263. The dock. Пристань.   *PR^yEE-stuhn^y.*

264. The cabin. Каюта.   *kah-YOO-tuh.*

265. The deck. Палуба.   *PAH-loo-buh.*

266. The gymnasium.

Гимнастический зал.
g^yeem-nah-ST^yEE-chih-sk^yee zahl.

267. The pool. Бассейн.   *bah-S^yEH͜EEN.*

268. The captain. Капитан.   *kuh-p^yee-TAHN.*

269. The purser.

Финансовый администратор.
f^yee-NAHN-suh-vï͜ee ahd-m^yee-n^yee-STRAH-tuhr.

270. The cabin steward (LIT.: **The person on corridor duty**).

Дежурный (F.: Дежурная) по коридору.
d^yih-ZHOOR-nï͜ee (F.: *d^yih-ZHOOR-nuh-yuh*)
puh-kuh-r^yee-DOH-roo.

AIRPLANE

271. I want [to make] [to cancel] a reservation.
Я хочу́ [заказа́ть] [сда́ть] биле́т.
*yah khah-CHOO [zuh-kah-ZAHT^y] [zdaht^y]
b^yee-L^yEHT.*

272. When is the next flight to [Kiev]?
Когда́ сле́дующий рейс на [Ки́ев]?
*kahg-DAH SL^yEH-doo-yoo-shhee r^yeh_ees
nah-[K^yEE-yihf]?*

273. When does the plane arrive in [Leningrad]?
Когда́ самолёт прибыва́ет в [Ленингра́д]?
*kahg-DAH suh-mah-L^yOHT pr^yee-bï-VAH-yiht
v[l^yih-n^yeen-GRAHT]?*

274. What kind of plane is used on that flight?
Како́й тип самолёта обслу́живает э́тот рейс?
*kah-KOY t^yeep suh-mah-L^yOH-tuh ahp-SLOO-zhï-
vuh-yiht EH-tuht r^yeh_ees?*

275. Will food be served?
Бу́дут ли корми́ть в самолёте?
BOO-doot-l^yee kahr-M^yEET^y fsuh-mah-L^yOH-t^yih?

276. May I confirm the reservation by telephone?
Мо́жно потверди́ть зака́з по телефо́ну?
*MOHZH-nuh puh-tv^yihr-D^yEET^y zah-KAHS
puh-t^yih-l^yih-FOH-noo?*

277. At what time should we check in [at the airport]?
Когда́ бу́дет регистра́ция [в аэропорту́]?
*kahg-DAH BOO-d^yiht r^yih-g^yih-STRAH-tsï-yuh
[vah-eh-ruh-pahr-TOO]?*

278. How long does it take to get to the airport from my hotel?
Как до́лго е́хать от гости́ницы до аэропо́рта?

kahk DOHL-guh YEH-khuht^y ahd-gah-ST^yEE-n^yee-tsï
dah-ah-eh-rah-POHR-tuh?

279. Is there bus service between the airport and the city?

Есть ли автобус от аэропорта до города?

YEHST^y-l^yee ahf-TOH-boos ah-tah-eh-rah-POHR-tuh
dah-GOH-ruh-duh?

280. Is that flight [nonstop] [direct]?

Этот рейс [беспосадочный] [прямой]?

EH-tuht r^yeh_ees [b^yihs-pah-SAH-duhch-nï_ee]
[pr^yih-MOY]?

281. Where does the plane stop en route?

Где самолёт делает посадку в пути?

gd^yeh suh-mah-L^yOHT D^yEH-luh-yiht pah-SAHT-koo
fpoo-T^yEE?

282. How long do we stop?

Как долго самолёт будет стоять?

kahk DOHL-guh suh-mah-L^yOHT BOO-d^yiht
stah-YAHT^y?

283. May I stop over in [Samarkand]?

Можно сделать остановку в [Самарканде]?

MOHZH-nuh ZD^yEH-luht^y ah-stah-NOHF-koo
f[suh-mahr-KAHN-d^yih]?

284. Is flight [number 22] on time (LIT.: proceeding according to schedule)?

Рейс [номер двадцать два] идёт по расписанию?

r^yeh_ees [NOH-m^yihr DVAHT-tsuht^y dvah] ee-D^yOHT
puh-ruhs-p^yee-SAH-n^yee-yoo?

285. How much baggage am I allowed?

Какой вес багажа разрешается провозить?

kah-KOY v^yehs buh-gah-ZHAH ruhz-r^yih-SHAH-yiht-
tsuh pruh-vah-Z^yEET^y?

286. How much per kilo for excess?
Ско́лько за ка́ждое кило́ сверх но́рмы?
*SKOHL>-kuh zah-KAHZH-duh-yuh k>ee-LOH
sv>ihrkh-NOHR-mï?*

287. May I carry this on board?
Мо́жно э́то взять на борт?
MOHZH-nuh EH-tuh vz>aht> nah-BOHRT?

288. Give me a seat [on the aisle].
Да́йте мне́ ме́сто [у прохо́да].
DAH＿EE-t>ih mn>eh M>EH-stuh [oo-prah-KHOH-duh].

289. —by a window.   —у окна́.   *—oo-ahk-NAH.*

290. —by the emergency exit.
—у запасно́го вы́хода.
—oo-zuh-pahs-NOH-vuh VÏ-khuh-duh.

291. May we board the plane now?
Мо́жно се́сть на самолёт сейча́с?
MOHZH-nuh s>ehst> nuh-suh-mah-L>OHT s>ih-CHAHS?

292. From which gate does my flight leave?
С како́го вы́хода поса́дка на мо́й ре́йс?
*skah-KOH-vuh VÏ-khuh-duh pah-SAHT-kuh nah-MOY
r>eh＿ees?*

293. Call the stewardess.
Позови́те стюарде́ссу.
puh-zah-V>EE-t>ih st>oo-ahr-DEHS-soo.

294. Fasten your seat belt.
Застегни́те привязны́е ремни́ (OR: Пристегни́те
ремни́).
*zuh-st>ihg-N>EE-t>ih pr>ee-v>ihz-NÏ-yih r>ihm-N>EE
(OR: pr>ee-st>ihg-N>EE-t>ih r>ihm-N>EE).*

295. May I smoke?
Мо́жно кури́ть?   *MOHZH-nuh koo-R>EET>?*

296. Is the flight [on time] [late]?

Рейс [идёт по расписа́нию] [опа́здывает]?

rʸeh‿ees [ee-DʸOHT puh-ruhs-pʸee-SAH-nʸee-yoo] [ah-PAHZ-dï-vuh-yiht]?

297. An announcement.

Объявле́ние. ahb-yihv-LʸEH-nʸee-yuh.

298. A boarding pass.

Поса́дочный тало́н.

pah-SAH-duhch-nï‿ee tah-LOHN.

TRAIN

299. When does the ticket office [open] [close]?

Когда́ [откро́ется] [закро́ется] биле́тная ка́сса?

kahg-DAH [aht-KROH-yiht-tsuh] [zah-KROH-yiht-tsuh] bʸee-LʸEHT-nuh-yuh KAHS-suh?

300. When is the next train for [Minsk]?

Когда́ отхо́дит сле́дующий по́езд в [Ми́нск]?

kahg-DAH aht-KHOH-dʸiht SLʸEH-doo-yoo-shhee POH-yihst v[mʸeensk]?

301. Is there [an earlier train]?

Есть ли [бо́лее ра́нний по́езд]?

YEHSTʸ-lʸee [BOH-lʸih-yih RAHN-nʸee POH-yihst]?

302. —a later train.

—бо́лее по́здний по́езд.

—BOH-lʸih-yih POHZ-nʸee POH-yihst.

303. —an express train.

—экспре́сс. —ehk-SPRʸEHS.

304. —a local train.

—при́городный по́езд.

—PRʸEE-ġuh-ruhd-nï‿ee POH-yihst.

305. From which track (OR: platform) does the train leave?

С како́го пути́ (OR: С како́й платфо́рмы) отхо́дит
по́езд?

skah-KOH-vuh poo-T^yEE (OR: *skah-KOY plaht-FOHR-
mï*) *aht-KHOH-d^yiht POH-yihst?*

306. Where can I see a timetable?*

Где́ мо́жно посмотре́ть расписа́ние?

*gd^yeh MOHZH-nuh puh-smah-TR^yEHT^y
ruhs-p^yee-SAH-n^yee-yuh?*

307. Does this train stop at [Rostov]?

Э́тот по́езд остана́вливается в [Росто́ве]?

*EH-tuht POH-yihst ah-stah-NAHV-l^yee-vuh-yiht-tsuh
v[rah-STOH-v^yih]?*

308. Is there time to get off?

Я успе́ю сойти́?   *yah oo-SP^yEH-yoo sah＿ee-T^yEE?*

309. When do we arrive?

Когда́ мы прибу́дем?

kahg-DAH mï pr^yee-BOO-d^yihm?

310. Is this seat taken?

Э́то ме́сто за́нято?   *EH-tuh M^yEH-stuh ZAH-n^yih-tuh?*

311. Am I disturbing you?

Я вам меша́ю?   *yah vahm m^yih-SHAH-yoo?*

312. Open the window.

Откро́йте окно́.   *aht-KROY-t^yih ahk-NOH.*

313. Close the door.

Закро́йте дверь.   *zah-KROY-t^yih dv^yehr^y.*

314. Where are we now?

Где́ мы сейча́с?   *gd^yeh mï s^yih-CHAHS?*

---

* Timetables are posted in all Soviet stations, but seldom
available for individual distribution.

315. Is the train on time?
Поезд идёт по расписанию?
POH-yihst ee-D^yOHT puh-ruhs-p^yee-SAH-n^yee-yoo?

316. How late are we?
На сколько времени мы опаздываем?
nah-SKOHL^y-kuh VR^yEH-m^yih-n^yee mï ah-PAHZ-dï-vuh-yihm?

317. The conductor.
Кондуктор. *kahn-DOOK-tuhr.*

318. The ticket-taker.
Проводник (F.: Проводница).
pruh-vahd-N^yEEK (F.: pruh-vahd-N^yEE-tsuh).

319. The ticket-checker.
Контролёр. *kuhn-trah-L^yOHR.*

320. The gate. Вход. *fkhoht.*

321. The information office (OR: **booth**).
Справочное бюро. *SPRAH-vuhch-nuh-yuh b^yoo-ROH.*

322. A one-way ticket.
Билет в один конец.
b^yee-L^yEHT vah-D^yEEN kah-N^yEHTS.

323. A round-trip ticket.
Билет в оба конца (OR: Билет туда и обратно).
b^yee-L^yEHT VOH-buh kahn-TSAH (OR: b^yee-L^yEHT too-DAH ee ah-BRAHT-nuh).

324. The railroad station (urban/rural).
Вокзал/станция. *vahg-ZAHL/STAHN-tsï-yuh.*

325. The waiting room.
Зал ожидания. *zahl ah-zhï-DAH-n^yee-yuh.*

326. The sleeping car.
Спальный вагон. *SPAHL^y-nï_ee vah-GOHN.*

327. A bedroom compartment (OR: roomette).
Купе́.   *koo-PEH.*

328. The smoking car.
Ваго́н для куря́щих.
vah-GOHN dl^{y}uh-koo-R^{y}AH-shheekh.

329. The dining car.
Ваго́н-рестора́н.   *vah-GOHN–r^{y}ih-stah-RAHN.*

BUS, TROLLEYBUS, SUBWAY, STREETCAR, MINIBUS

330. Where does [the streetcar] [the trolleybus] stop?
Где́ остана́вливается [трамва́й] [тролле́йбус]?
*gd^{y}eh ah-stah-NAHV-l^{y}ee-vuh-yiht-tsuh
[trahm-VAH ⌣ EE] [trah-L^{y}EH ⌣ EE-boos]?*

331. How often does the [bus] [minibus] run?
Ка́к ча́сто остана́вливается [авто́бус]
[маршру́тное такси́]?
*kahk CHAH-stuh ah-stah-NAHV-l^{y}ee-vuh-yiht-tsuh
[ahf-TOH-boos] [mahrsh-ROOT-nuh-yuh tahk-S^{y}EE]?*

332. [Which bus] goes to [Smolensk]?
[Како́й авто́бус] идёт в [Смоле́нск]?
*[kah-KOY ahf-TOH-boos] ee-D^{y}OHT
f[smah-L^{y}EHNSK]?*

333. How much is the fare?
Ско́лько сто́ит прое́зд?
SKOHL^y-kuh STOH-yiht prah-YEHST?

334. Do you go near [Gorky Street]?
Вы́ проезжа́ете ми́мо [у́лицы Го́рького]?
*vï pruh-yih-ZHHAH-yih-t^{y}ih M^{y}EE-muh [OO-l^{y}ee-tsï
GOHR^y-kuh-vuh]?*

335. I want to get off [at the next stop].

Я хочу сойти [на следующей остановке].

yah khah-CHOO sah ͜ ee-T ʸEE [nah-SL ʸEH-doo-yoo-shhih ͜ ee ah-stah-NOHF-k ʸih].

336. —right here. —здесь. —*zd ʸehs ʸ.*

337. Please tell me where to get off.

Прошу сказать мне, где сойти.

prah-SHOO skah-ZAHT ʸ mn ʸeh, gd ʸeh sah ͜ ee-T ʸEE.

338. Will I have to change?

Надо пересесть?

NAH-duh p ʸih-r ʸih-S ʸEHST ʸ?

339. Where do we transfer?

Где мы должны пересесть?

gd ʸeh mï dahlzh-N Ї p ʸih-r ʸih-S ʸEHST ʸ?

340. The driver. Водитель. *vah-D ʸEE-t ʸihl ʸ.*

341. 5-kopeck piece (for subway, bus).*

Пятикопеечная монета.

p ʸih-t ʸee-kah-P ʸEH-yihch-nuh-yuh mah-N ʸEH-tuh.

342. 4-kopeck piece (for trolleybus).*

Четырёхкопеечная монета.

chih-tï-R ʸOHKH-kah-P ʸEH-yihch-nuh-yuh mah-N ʸEH-tuh.

343. 3-kopeck piece (for streetcar).*

Трёхкопеечная монета.

TR ʸOHKH-kah-P ʸEH-yihch-nuh-yuh mah-N ʸEH-tuh.

344. Coupon (for bus).

Талон на проезд. *tah-LOHN nah-prah-YEHST.*

---

* Though these fares remained stable for many years, there is of course a possibility that they have changed.

345. Monthly pass (for all city transportation).
Ежемéсячный билéт.
yih-zhï-MʸEH-sʸihch-nĭ_ee bʸee-LʸEHT.

346. The bus stop.
Останóвка автóбуса.
ah-stah-NOHF-kuh ahf-TOH-boo-suh.

347. Where is [the subway]?
Гдé [метрó]? *gdʸeh [mʸih-TROH]?*

348. Next station, [Sverdlov Square].
Слéдующая — [плóщадь Свердлóва].
*SLʸEH-doo-yoo-shhuh-yuh — [PLOH-shhihtʸ
svʸihrd-LOH-vuh].*

349. Careful, the doors are closing.
Осторóжно, двéри закрывáются.
*ah-stah-ROHZH-nuh, DVʸEH-rʸee zuh-krï-VAH-yoot-
tsuh.*

350. The train goes as far as [University] station.
Пóезд слéдует до стáнции [Университéт].
*POH-yihst SLʸEH-doo-yiht dah-STAHN-tsï-yee
[oo-nʸee-vʸihr-sʸee-TʸEHT].*

351. Last stop; please vacate all cars.
Пóезд дáльше не идёт; прóсьба освободúть вагóны.
*POH-yihst DAHLʸ-shï nʸih-ee-DʸOHT; PROHZʸ-buh
ah-svuh-bah-DʸEETʸ vah-GOH-nï.*

TAXI

352. Call a taxi for me.
Вы́зовите мнé таксú.
VÏ-zuh-vʸee-tʸih mnʸeh tahk-SʸEE.

353. Are you free, (driver)?

(Води́тель), вы свобо́дны?

(*vah-D^yEE-t^yihl^y*), *vï svah-BOHD-nï?*

354. What do you charge [per hour]?

Ско́лько вы возьмёте [за час]?

SKOHL^y-kuh vï vahz^y-M^yOH-t^yih [zah-CHAHS]?

355. —per kilometer.

—за киломе́тр. —*zah-k^yee-lah-M^yEH-tuhr.*

356. —per day. —за́ день. —*ZAH-d^yihn^y.*

357. Take me to this address.

Отвези́те меня́ по э́тому а́дресу.

aht-v^yih-Z^yEE-t^yih m^yih-N^yAH pah-EH-tuh-moo AH-dr^yih-soo.

358. How much will the ride cost?

Ско́лько э́тот прое́зд бу́дет сто́ить?

SKOHL^y-kuh EH-tuht prah-YEHST BOO-d^yiht STOH-yiht^y?

359. How long will it take to get there?

Ско́лько вре́мени займёт э́та пое́здка?

SKOHL^y-kuh VR^yEH-m^yih-n^yee zah⁀ee-M^yOHT EH-tuh pah-YEHST-kuh?

360. Drive us around [for one hour].

Повези́те нас [час] по го́роду.

pah-v^yih-Z^yEE-t^yih nahs [chahs] pah-GOH-ruh-doo.

361. Please drive [more carefully] [more slowly].

Прошу́ вас е́хать [осторо́жнее] [поме́дленнее].

prah-SHOO vahs YEH-khuht^y [ah-stah-ROHZH-n^yih-yih] [pah-M^yEH-dl^yihn-n^yih-yih].

362. I am [not] in a great hurry.

Я [не] о́чень спешу́.

yah [n^yih]-OH-chihn^y sp^yih-SHOO.

363. Stop here.

Остановитесь здесь.

ah-stuh-nah-V^yEE-t^yihs^y zd^yehs^y.

364. Wait for me here.

Подождите меня здесь.

puh-dahzh-D^yEE-t^yih m^yih-N^yAH zd^yehs^y.

365. I will return in [five minutes].

Я вернусь через [пять минут].

yah v^yihr-NOOS^y chih-r^yihs-[P^yAHT^y m^yee-NOOT].

366. Keep the change.

Возьмите сдачу себе.

vahz^y-M^yEE-t^yih ZDAH-choo s^yih-B^yEH.

367. The taxi stand.

Стоянка такси.   *stah-YAHN-kuh tahk-S^yEE.*

368. The taxi meter.

Таксометр.   *tahk-SOH-m^yih-tuhr.*

RENTING AUTOS (AND OTHER VEHICLES)

369. What kind [of cars] do you have?

Какие у вас марки [автомобиля]?*

kah-K^yEE-yih oo-VAHS MAHR-k^yee [ahf-tuh-mah-B^yEE-l^yuh]?

370. I have an international driver's license.

У меня международные водительские права.

oo-m^yih-N^yAH m^yihzh-doo-nah-ROHD-nï-yih vah-D^yEE-t^yihl^y-sk^yee-yih prah-VAH.

---

* Автомобиль (*ahf-tuh-mah-B^yEEL^y*) corresponds to the English word "automobile"; the word машина (*mah-SHĬ-nuh*) is more common in colloquial speech.

371. What is the rate [per day]?

Ско́лько сто́ит аре́нда [за́ день]?

*SKOHL*ʸ*-kuh STOH-yiht ah-R*ʸ*EHN-duh [ZAH-d*ʸ*ihn*ʸ*]?*

372. How much additional [per kilometer]?

Кака́я дополни́тельная пла́та [за киломе́тр]?

*kah-KAH-yuh duh-pahl-N*ʸ*EE-t*ʸ*ihl*ʸ*-nuh-yuh PLAH-tuh*
*[zuh-k*ʸ*ee-lah-M*ʸ*EH-tuhr]?*

373. Are gas and oil (also) included?

Бензи́н и ма́сло (то́же) включены́ в це́ну?

*b*ʸ*ihn-Z*ʸ*EEN ee MAHS-luh (TOH-zhĭ) fkl*ʸ*oo-chih-NЇ*
FTSEH-noo?

374. Does the insurance policy cover [personal liability]?

Включена́ ли в страхо́вку [компенса́ция же́ртвам в
слу́чае ава́рии]?

*fkl*ʸ*oo-chih-NAH-l*ʸ*ee fstrah-KHOHF-koo [kuhm-p*ʸ*ihn-*
SAH-tsĭ-yuh ZHEHRT-vuhm FSLOO-chih-yih
*ah-VAH-r*ʸ*ee-yee]?*

375. —property damage.

—компенса́ция за поврежде́ние иму́щества.

*—kuhm-p*ʸ*ihn-SAH-tsĭ-yuh zuh-puh-vr*ʸ*ihzh-D*ʸ*EH-*
*n*ʸ*ee-yuh ee-MOO-shhih-stvuh.*

376. —collision.

—компенса́ция за ремо́нт автомоби́ля в слу́чае
столкнове́ния.

*—kuhm-p*ʸ*ihn-SAH-tsĭ-yuh zuh-r*ʸ*ih-MOHNT ahf-tuh-*
*mah-B*ʸ*EE-l*ʸ*uh FSLOO-chih-yih stuhlk-nah-V*ʸ*EH-*
*n*ʸ*ee-yuh.*

377. Are the papers in order?

Всё докуме́нты в поря́дке?

*fs*ʸ*eh duh-koo-M*ʸ*EHN-tĭ fpah-R*ʸ*AHT-k*ʸ*ih?*

378. I am not familiar with this car.
Я не знако́м (F.: знако́ма) с э́той маши́ной.
*yah nʸih-znah-KOHM (F.: znah-KOH-muh) SEH-tuh ̲ee
mah-SHĬ-nuh ̲ee.*

379. Explain [this dial].
Объясни́те [э́тот цифербла́т].
ahb-yihs-NʸEE-tʸih [EH-tuht tsï-fʸihr-BLAHT].

380. —this mechanism.
—э́тот механи́зм.   —*EH-tuht mʸih-khah-NʸEE-zuhm.*

381. Show me how [the heater] operates.
Покажи́те мне́, ка́к рабо́тает [обогрева́тель].
*puh-kah-ZHĬ-tʸih mnʸeh, kahk rah-BOH-tuh-yiht
[ah-buh-grʸih-VAH-tʸihl].*

382. Will some one pick the car up at the hotel?
Кто́-нибудь заберёт маши́ну от гости́ницы?
*KTOH-nʸee-bootʸ zuh-bʸih-RʸOHT mah-SHĬ-noo
aht-gah-STʸEE-nʸee-tsï?*

383. Is the office open all night?
Конто́ра рабо́тает кру́глые су́тки?
*kahn-TOH-ruh rah-BOH-tuh-yiht KROOG-lï-yih
SOOT-kʸee?*

384. The bicycle.
Велисопе́д.   *vʸih-lʸee-sah-PʸEHT.*

385. The motorcycle.
Мотоци́кл.   *muh-tah-TSĬ-kuhl.*

386. The motor scooter.
Моторо́ллер.   *muh-tah-ROH-lʸihr.*

387. The horse and carriage.
Ло́шадь с коля́ской.
LOH-shuhtʸ skah-LʸAHS-kuh ̲ee.

AUTO: DIRECTIONS

388. What is the name of [this city]?
Как называется [этот город]?
kahk nuh-zï-VAH-yiht-tsuh [EH-tuht GOH-ruht]?

389. How far [to the next town]?
Как далеко [до следующего города]?
kahk duh-lʸih-KOH [dah-SLʸEH-doo-yoo-shhih-vuh GOH-ruh-duh]?

390. Where does [this road] lead?
Куда ведёт [эта дорога]?
koo-DAH vʸih-DʸOHT [EH-tuh dah-ROH-guh]?

391. Are there road signs?
Есть ли дорожные указатели?
YEHSTʸ-lʸee dah-ROHZH-nï-yih oo-kah-ZAH-tʸih-lʸee?

392. Is the road [paved]?
Дорога [мощёная]?
dah-ROH-guh [mah-SHHOH-nuh-yuh]?

393. —well-paved (LIT.: **even**).
—ровная. *—ROHV-nuh-yuh.*

394. Show me the easiest way.
Покажите мне наилучший путь.
puh-kah-ZHЇ-tʸih mnʸeh nuh-ee-LOOCH-shï̈_ee pootʸ.

395. Show it to me on this road map.
Покажите мне его на этой дорожной карте.
puh-kah-ZHЇ-tʸih mnʸeh yih-VOH nah-EH-tuh_ee dah-ROHZH-nuh_ee KAHR-tʸih.

396. Can I avoid heavy traffic?
Можно избежать большого движения?
MOHZH-nuh eez-bʸih-ZHAHTʸ bahlʸ-SHOH-vuh dvʸee-ZHEH-nʸee-yuh?

397. May I park here [for a while]?
Мо́жно здѣсь поста́вить маши́ну [на вре́мя]?
MOHZH-nuh zd'ehs' pah-STAH-v'eet' mah-SHĬ-noo [nah-VR'EH-m'uh]?

398. —overnight. —на́ ночь. —*NAH-nuhch.*

399. The approach. Подъѣзд. *pahd-YEHST.*

400. The expressway. Шоссе́. *shahs-SEH.*

401. The fork. Развилка. *rahz-V'EEL-kuh.*

402. The major road.
Гла́вная доро́га. *GLAHV-nuh-yuh dah-ROH-guh.*

403. The garage. Гара́ж. *gah-RAHSH.*

404. The auto repair shop.
Авторемо́нтная мастерска́я.
ahf-tuh-r'ih-MOHNT-nuh-yuh muh-st'ihr-SKAH-yuh.

405. The gas station.
Бензоколо́нка (OR: Автозапра́вочная ста́нция, ABBREV. АЗС).
b'ihn-zuh-kah-LOHN-kuh (OR: *ahf-tuh-zah-PRAH-vuhch-nuh-yuh STAHN-tsĭ-yuh*).

406. The parking lot.
Ме́сто стоя́нки автомоби́лей.
M'EH-stuh stah-YAHN-k'ee ahf-tuh-mah-B'EE-l'ih_ee.

407. The traffic light. Светофо́р. *sv'ih-tah-FOHR.*

408. The stop sign.
Сигна́л «Стоп». *s'eeg-NAHL "stohp".*

AUTO: HELP ON THE ROAD

409. My car has broken down.
У меня́ слома́лась маши́на.
oo-m'ih-N'AH slah-MAH-luhs' mah-SHĬ-nuh.

410. Call a mechanic (in person/by phone).

Вы́зовите меха́ника/Позвони́те меха́нику.

VĬ-zuh-vᵉee-tᵉih mᵉih-KHAH-nᵉee-kuh/puh-zvah-
NᵉEE-tᵉih mᵉih-KHAH-nᵉee-koo.

411. Help me push [the car] to the side.

Помоги́те мне́ откати́ть [маши́ну] от доро́ги.

*puh-mah-GᵉEE-tᵉih mn*ᵉ*eh aht-kah-TᵉEETᵉ*
[mah-SHĬ-noo] ahd-dah-ROH-gᵉee.

412. Push me.

Толкни́те меня́. *tahlk-NᵉEE-tᵉih mᵉih-NᵉAH.*

413. May I borrow [a jack]?

Мо́жно у ва́с заня́ть [домкра́т]?

MOHZH-nuh oo-VAHS zah-NᵉAHTᵉ [dahm-KRAHT]?

414. Change the tire.

Смени́те ши́ну. *smᵉih-NᵉEE-tᵉih SHĬ-noo.*

415. My car is stuck [in the mud] [in the ditch].

Моя́ маши́на застря́ла [в грязи́] [в кана́ве].

mah-YAH mah-SHĬ-nuh zah-STRᵉAH-luh
[vgrᵉih-ZᵉEE] [ʃkah-NAH-vᵉih].

416. Drive me to the nearest gas station.

Отвези́те меня́ на ближа́йшую бензоколо́нку
(OR: автозапра́вочную ста́нцию).

aht-vᵉih-ZᵉEE-tᵉih mᵉih-NᵉAH nuh-blᵉee-ZHAN‿EE-
shoo-yoo bᵉihn-zuh-kah-LOHN-koo (OR: ahf-tuh-zah-
PRAH-vuhch-noo-yoo STAHN-tsĭ-yoo).

AUTO: GAS STATION AND REPAIR SHOP

417. Give me [twenty] liters [of regular gasoline].

Налейте мне [двадцать] литров [А-76].

*nah-L*ʸ*EH͜EE-t*ʸ*ih mn*ʸ*eh [DVAHT-tsuht*ʸ*] L*ʸ*EE-truhf [ah S*ʸ*EHM*ʸ*-d*ʸ*ih-s*ʸ*iht shehst*ʸ*].*

418. —of premium gasoline.

—А-93.   *—ah d*ʸ*ih-v*ʸ*ih-NOHS-tuh tr*ʸ*ee.*

419. —of diesel fuel.

—дизельного топлива.

*—D*ʸ*EE-z*ʸ*ihl*ʸ*-nuh-vuh TOH-pl*ʸ*ee-vuh.*

420. Fill it up.

Наполните бак.   *nah-POHL-n*ʸ*ee-t*ʸ*ih bahk.*

421. Check the oil.

Проверьте масло.   *prah-V*ʸ*EHR*ʸ*-t*ʸ*ih MAHS-luh.*

422. Lubricate the car.

Смажьте машину.   *SMAHSH-t*ʸ*ih mah-SHĬ-noo.*

423. [Light] [medium] [heavy] oil.

[Лёгкое] [среднее] [тяжёлое] масло.

*[L*ʸ*OHKH-kuh-yuh] [SR*ʸ*EHD-n*ʸ*uh-yuh] [t*ʸ*ih-ZHOH-luh-yuh] MAHS-luh.*

424. Put water in the radiator.

Долейте воду в радиатор.

*dah-L*ʸ*EH͜EE-t*ʸ*ih VOH-doo vruh-d*ʸ*ee-AH-tuhr.*

425. Recharge the battery.

Перезарядите аккумулятор.

*p*ʸ*ih-r*ʸ*ih-zuh-r*ʸ*ih-D*ʸ*EE-t*ʸ*ih ah-koo-moo-L*ʸ*AH-tuhr.*

426. Clean the windshield.

Вымойте ветровое стекло.

*VĬ-muh͜ee-t*ʸ*ih v*ʸ*ih-trah-VOH-yuh st*ʸ*ih-KLOH.*

427. Adjust the brakes.

Отрегули́руйте тормоза́.

aht-r^{y}ih-goo-L^{y}EE-roo＿ee-t^{y}ih tuhr-mah-ZAH.

428. Check the tire pressure.

Прове́рьте давле́ние в ши́нах.

prah-V^{y}EHR^y-t^{y}ih dahv-L^{y}EH-n^{y}ee-yuh FSHЍ-nuhkh.

429. Repair the flat tire.

Почини́те ши́ну. *puh-chee-N^{y}EE-t^{y}ih SHЍ-noo.*

430. Could you wash it [now]?

Вы мо́жете помы́ть её [сейча́с]?

vï MOH-zhuh-t^{y}ih pah-MЍT^y yih-YOH [s^{y}ih-CHAHS]?

431. How long must we wait?

Ка́к до́лго на́м на́до жда́ть?

kahk DOHL-guh nahm NAH-duh zhdaht^y?

432. The motor overheats.

Мото́р перегрева́ется.

mah-TOHR p^{y}ih-r^{y}ih-gr^{y}ih-VAH-yiht-tsuh.

433. Is there a leak?

Е́сть ли уте́чка? *YEHST^y-l^{y}ee oo-T^{y}EHCH-kuh?*

434. It makes a noise.

Она́ даёт посторо́нний шу́м.

ah-NAH dah-YOHT puh-stah-ROHN-n^{y}ee shoom.

435. The lights do not work.

Фа́ры не рабо́тают. *FAH-rï n^{y}ih-rah-BOH-tuh-yoot.*

436. The car does not start.

Маши́на не заво́дится.

mah-SHЍ-nuh n^{y}ih-zah-VOH-d^{y}iht-tsuh.

PARTS OF THE CAR
(AND AUTO EQUIPMENT)

437. Accelerator.
Акселера́тор. *ahk-s^{y}ih-l^{y}ih-RAH-tuhr.*

438. Air filter.
Возду́шный фи́льтр.
vahz-DOOSH-nï͟_ee F^{y}EEL^y-tuhr.

439. Alcohol. Спи́рт. *sp^{y}eert.*

440. Antifreeze. Антифри́з. *ahn-t^{y}ee-FR^{y}EES.*

441. Axle. Ось. *ohs^y.*

442. Battery. Аккумуля́тор. *ah-koo-moo-L^{y}AH-tuhr.*

443. Bolt. Бо́лт. *bohlt.*

444. Foot brake.
Ножно́й то́рмоз. *nahzh-NOY TOHR-muhs.*

445. Hand (OR: **Parking) brake.**
Ручно́й (OR: Стоя́ночный) то́рмоз.
rooch-NOY (OR: *stah-YAH-nuhch-nï͟_ee) TOHR-muhs.*

446. Bumper. Ба́мпер. *BAHM-p^{y}ihr.*

447. Carburetor. Карбюра́тор. *kahr-b^{y}oo-RAH-tuhr.*

448. Chassis. Шасси́. *shahs-S^{y}EE.*

449. Choke (automatic).
(Автомати́ческая) возду́шная засло́нка.
*(ahf-tuh-mah-T^{y}EE-chih-skuh-yuh) vahz-DOOSH-nuh-yuh
zah-SLOHN-kuh.*

450. Clutch. Сцепле́ние. *stsï-PL^{y}EH-n^{y}ee-yuh.*

451. Cylinder. Цили́ндр. *tsï-L^{y}EEN-duhr.*

452. Dashboard. Щито́к. *shhee-TOHK.*

453. Differential.
Дифференциа́л. *d^{y}ee-f^{y}ih-r^{y}ihn-tsï-AHL.*

454. Door. Дверца. *DV^yEHR-tsuh.*

455. Electrical system.
Электрическая система.
eh-l^yihk-TR^yEE-chih-skuh-yuh s^yee-ST^yEH-muh.

456. Engine (OR: **Motor**).
Двигатель (OR: Мотор).
DV^yEE-guh-t^yihl^y (OR: *mah-TOHR*).

457. Exhaust pipe.
Выхлопная труба. *vï-khlahp-NAH-yuh troo-BAH.*

458. Exterior. Внешность. *VN^yEHSH-nuhst^y.*

459. Fan. Вентилятор. *v^yihn-t^yee-L^yAH-tuhr.*

460. Fan belt.
Ремень вентилятора.
r^yih-M^yEHN^y v^yihn-t^yee-L^yAH-tuh-ruh.

461. Fender. Крыло. *krï-LOH.*

462. Flashlight.
Электрический фонарь.
eh-l^yihk-TR^yEE-chih-sk^yee fah-NAHR^y.

463. Fuel pump.
Топливый насос (OR: Бензопомпа).
TOH-pl^yee-vï͟_ee nah-SOHS (OR: *b^yihn-zah-POHM-puh*).

464. Fuse.
Предохранитель. *pr^yih-duh-khrah-N^yEE-t^yihl^y.*

465. Gas tank. Бензобак. *b^yihn-zah-BAHK.*

466. Gear shift.
Рычаг переключения скоростей.
rï-CHAHK p^yih-r^yih-kl^yoo-CHEH-n^yee-yuh skuh-rahs-T^yEH͟_EE.

467. [First] [second] gear.
[Первая] [вторая] скорость.
[P^yEHR-vuh-yuh] [ftah-RAH-yuh] SKOH-ruhst^y.

468. [Third] [fourth] gear.
[Тре́тья] [четвёртая] ско́рость.
[*TR^yEHT^y-yuh*] [*chiht-V^yOHR-tuh-yuh*] *SKOH-ruhst^y*.

469. Reverse gear.
За́дний хо́д. *ZAHD-n^yee khoht*.

470. Neutral gear. Нейтра́ль. *n^yih＿ee-TRAHL^y*.

471. Grease. Сма́зка. *SMAHS-kuh*.

472. Generator. Генера́тор. *g^yih-n^yih-RAH-tuhr*.

473. Hammer. Молото́к. *muh-lah-TOHK*.

474. Hood. Капо́т. *kah-POHT*.

475. Horn.
Звуково́й сигна́л (OR: Гудо́к).
zvoo-kah-VOY s^yeeg-NAHL (OR: *goo-DOHK*).

476. Horsepower.
Лошади́ная си́ла. *luh-shï-D^yEE-nuh-yuh S^yEE-luh*.

477. Ignition key.
Ключ зажига́ния. *kl^yooch zuh-zhï-GAH-n^yee-yuh*.

478. Inner tube. Ка́мера. *KAH-m^yih-ruh*.

479. Instrument panel.
Пане́ль управле́ния.
pah-N^yEHL^y oo-prahv-L^yEH-n^yee-yuh.

480. License plate.
Номерно́й зна́к. *nuh-m^yihr-NOY znahk*.

481. Light. Ла́мпочка. *LAHM-puhch-kuh*.

482. Parking light.
Подфа́рник. *paht-FAHR-n^yeek*.

483. Brake light.
Тормозно́й фона́рь. *tuhr-mahz-NOY fah-NAHR^y*.

484. Taillight.
За́дний фона́рь. *ZAHD-n^yee fah-NAHR^y*.

485. Rear-view mirror.
Заднее зеркало. *ZAHD-nʸih-yih ZʸEHR-kuh-luh.*

486. Side-view mirror.
Боковое зеркало. *buh-kah-VOH-yuh ZʸEHR-kuh-luh.*

487. Muffler. Глушитель. *gloo-SHĬ-tʸihlʸ.*

488. Nail. Гвоздь. *gvohstʸ.*

489. Nut. Гайка. *GAH _ EE-kuh.*

490. Pedal. Педаль. *pʸih-DAHLʸ.*

491. Pliers. Плоскогубцы. *pluh-skah-GOOP-tsï.*

492. Radiator. Радиатор. *ruh-dʸee-AH-tuhr.*

493. Radio. Радио. *RAH-dʸee-oh.*

494. Rags. Тряпки. *TRʸAHP-kʸee.*

495. Rope. Канат. *kah-NAHT.*

496. Screw. Винт. *vʸeent.*

497. Screwdriver. Отвёртка. *aht-VʸOHRT-kuh.*

498. Automatic shift.
Автоматическое переключение.
ahf-tuh-mah-TʸEE-chih-skuh-yuh pʸih-rʸih-klʸoo-CHEH-nʸee-yuh.

499. Hand shift.
Ручное переключение.
rooch-NOH-yuh pʸih-rʸih-klʸoo-CHEH-nʸee-yuh.

500. Shock absorber.
Амортизатор. *ah-muhr-tʸee-ZAH-tuhr.*

501. Skid chains. Цепи. *TSEH-pʸee.*

502. Snow tires.
Шины для снега. *SHĬ-nï dlʸah-SNʸEH-guh.*

503. Spark plugs. Свечи. *SVʸEH-chee.*

504. Speedometer. Спидо́метр. *sp^yee-DOH-m^yih-tuhr.*

505. Spring. Рессо́ра. *r^yih-SOH-ruh.*

506. Starter. Ста́ртер. *STAHR-t^yihr.*

507. Steering wheel. Руль. *rool^y.*

508. Tire. Ши́на. *SHĬ-nuh.*

509. Spare tire.
Запасно́е колесо́. *zuh-pahs-NOH-yuh kuh-l^yih-SOH.*

510. Tubeless tire.
Беска́мерная ши́на.
b^yihs-KAH-m^yihr-nuh-yuh SHĬ-nuh.

511. Tire pump.
Насо́с для шин. *nah-SOHS dl^yah-SHĬN.*

512. Tools. Инструме́нты. *een-stroo-M^yEHN-tï.*

513. Automatic transmission.
Автомати́ческая переда́ча.
ahf-tuh-mah-T^yEE-chih-skuh-yuh p^yih-r^yih-DAH-chuh.

514. Standard (OR: Manual) transmission.
Станда́ртная (OR: Ручна́я) переда́ча.
*stahn-DAHRT-nuh-yuh (OR: rooch-NAH-yuh)
p^yih-r^yih-DAH-chuh.*

515. Trunk. Бага́жник. *bah-GAHZH-n^yeek.*

516. Turn signal.
Указа́тель поворо́та.
oo-kah-ZAH-t^yihl^y puh-vah-ROH-tuh.

517. Valve. Кла́пан. *KLAH-puhn.*

518. Water-cooling system.
Систе́ма водяно́го охлажде́ния.
*s^yee-ST^yEH-muh vuh-d^yih-NOH-vuh ah-khlahzh-
D^yEH-n^yee-yuh.*

519. Front wheel.

Переднее колесо.

p^yih-R^yEHD-n^yuh-yuh kuh-l^yih-SOH.

520. Rear wheel.

Заднее колесо.   *ZAHD-n^yih-yih kuh-l^yih-SOH.*

521. Windshield wiper.

Стеклоочиститель (OR: Дворник).

st^yih-klah-ah-chee-ST^yEE-t^yihl^y (OR: *DVOHR-n^yeek*).

522. Wrench.

Гаечный ключ.   *GAH-yihch-nï＿ee kl^yooch.*

MAIL

523. Where is [the post office]?

Где [почта (OR: почтовое отделение)]?

gd^yeh [POHCH-tuh (OR: *pahch-TOH-vuh-yuh ahd-d^yih-L^yEH-n^yee-yuh*)]?

524. —a mailbox.

—почтовый ящик.   *—pahch-TOH-vï＿ee YAH-shheek.*

525. To which window should I go?

В какое окно следует обратиться?

*fkah-KOH-yuh ahk-NOH SL^yEH-doo-yiht
ah-brah-T^yEET-tsuh?*

526. I want to send this letter [by surface mail].

Я хочу послать это письмо [простой почтой].

*yah khah-CHOO pah-SLAHT^y EH-tuh p^yees^y-MOH
[prah-STOY POHCH-tuh＿ee].*

527. —by airmail.

—авиапочтой.   *—AH-v^yee-ah-POHCH-tuh＿ee.*

528. —by special delivery.
—со сро́чной доста́вкой.
—*sah-SROHCH-nuh ̮ee dah-STAHF-kuh ̮ee.*

529. —by registered mail, reply requested.
—заказно́й по́чтой с уведомле́нием.
—*zuh-kahz-NOY POHCH-tuh ̮ee soo-v^yih-dahm-L^yEH-n^yee-yihm.*

530. I want to send this parcel.
Я хочу́ посла́ть э́ту посы́лку.
yah khah-CHOO pah-SLAHT^y EH-too pah-SÏL-koo.

531. How much postage do I need to send [this postcard]?
На каку́ю су́мму мне́ нужны́ ма́рки чтобы посла́ть [э́ту откры́тку]?
nah-kah-KOO-yoo SOOM-moo mn^yeh noozh-NÏ MAHR-k^yee SHTOH-bï pah-SLAHT^y [EH-too aht-KRÏT-koo]?

532. The package contains [printed matter].
Посы́лка соде́ржит [печа́тный материа́л].
pah-SÏL-kuh sah-D^yEHR-zhït [p^yih-CHAHT-nï ̮ee muh-t^yih-r^yee-AHL].

533. —fragile material.
—хру́пкий материа́л.
—*KHROOP-k^yee muh-t^yih-r^yee-AHL.*

534. I want to insure this for [25 rubles].
Я хочу́ застрахова́ть э́то на [два́дцать пя́ть рубле́й].
yah khah-CHOO zuh-struh-khah-VAHT^y EH-tuh nah-[DVAHT-tsuht^y p^yaht^y roo-BL^yEH ̮EE].

535. Will this go out [today]?
Э́то отпра́вится [сего́дня]?
EH-tuh aht-PRAH-v^yeet-tsuh [s^yih-VOHD-n^yuh]?

536. Give me ten stamps [for airmail letters to the United States].

Дáйте мнé дéсять мáрок [для áвиапи́сем в Соединён-ные Штáты].

*DAH__EE-t*y*ih mn*y*eh D*y*EH-s*y*iht*y* MAH-ruhk [dl*y*ah-AH-v*y*ee-ah-P*y*EE-s*y*ihm fsuh-yih-d*y*ih-N*y*OHN-nï-yih SHTAH-tï].*

537. Where can I get (LIT.: send off) a money order?

Гдé мóжно отпрáвить дéнежный перевóд?

*gd*y*eh MOHZH-nuh aht-PRAH-v*y*eet*y* D*y*EH-n*y*ihzh-nï__ee p*y*ih-r*y*ih-VOHT?*

538. Please forward my mail to [Kiev].

Прошý пересла́ть мою́ по́чту в [Ки́ев].

*prah-SHOO p*y*ih-r*y*ih-SLAHT*y* mah-YOO POHCH-too f[K*y*EE-yihf].*

539. The American Express office will hold my mail.

Контóра «Амéрикан экспрéсс» бýдет получáть пóчту для меня́.

*kahn-TOH-ruh "ah-MEH-r*y*ee-kuhn ehk-SPR*y*EHS" BOO-d*y*iht pah-loo-CHAHT*y* POHCH-too dl*y*uh-m*y*ih-N*y*AH.*

TELEGRAM

540. I would like to send [a telegram].

Я хотéл (F.: хотéла) бы посла́ть [телегра́мму].

*yah khah-T*y*EHL (F.: khah-T*y*EH-luh)-bï pah-SLAHT*y* [t*y*ih-l*y*ih-GRAHM-moo].*

541. —a night letter.

—обы́чную телегра́мму.

*—ah-BÏCH-noo-yoo t*y*ih-l*y*ih-GRAHM-moo.*

542. —a cablegram.

—каблогра́мму. —*kuh-blah-GRAHM-moo.*

543. What is the rate per word?

Ско́лько сто́ит сло́во?

SKOHL^y-kuh STOH-yiht SLOH-vuh?

544. What is the minimum charge?

Кака́я минима́льная опла́та?

kah-KAH-yuh m^{y}ee-n^{y}ee-MAHL^y-nuh-yuh ah-PLAH-tuh?

545. When will a night letter reach [London]?

Когда́ обы́чная телегра́мма придёт в [Ло́ндон]?

*kahg-DAH ah-B$\breve{I}$CH-nuh-yuh t^{y}ih-l^{y}ih-GRAHM-muh
    pr^{y}ee-D^{y}OHT v[LOHN-duhn]?*

TELEPHONE

546. May I use the telephone?

Мо́жно позвони́ть по э́тому телефо́ну?

*MOHZH-nuh puh-zvah-N^{y}EET^y pah-EH-tuh-moo
    t^{y}ih-l^{y}ih-FOH-noo?*

547. Dial this number for me.

Набери́те э́тот но́мер для меня́.

*nuh-b^{y}ih-R^{y}EE-t^{y}ih EH-tuht NOH-m^{y}ihr dl^{y}uh-
    m^{y}ih-N^{y}AH.*

548. Operator, get me this number.

Коммута́тор, соедини́те меня́ с э́тим но́мером.

*kuh-moo-TAH-tuhr, suh-yih-d^{y}ih-N^{y}EE-t^{y}ih m^{y}ih-N^{y}AH
    SEH-t^{y}eem NOH-m^{y}ih-ruhm.*

549. Call me at this number.

Позвони́те мне́ по э́тому телефо́ну.

*puh-zvah-N^{y}EE-t^{y}ih mn^{y}eh pah-EH-tuh-moo t^{y}ih-l^{y}ih-
    FOH-noo.*

550. My (telephone) number is [139-14-96].

Мой номер (телефона) — [сто тридцать девять, четырнадцать, девяноста шесть].

moy NOH-m^yihr (t^yih-l^yih-FOH-nuh) — [stoh TR^yEET-tsuht^y D^yEH-v^yiht^y, chih-TÏR-nuht-tsuht^y, d^yih-v^yih-NOH-stuh shehst^y].

551. How much is a long-distance call to [Paris]?

Сколько стоит телефонный разговор с [Парижем]?

SKOHL^y-kuh STOH-yiht t^yih-l^yih-FOHN-nï_ee ruhz-gah-VOHR s[pah-R^yEE-zhuhm]?

552. What is the charge for the first three minutes?

Сколько стоят первые три минуты?

SKOHL^y-kuh STOH-yuht P^yEHR-vï-yih tr^yee m^yee-NOO-tï?

553. I want to reverse the charges.

Я хочу, чтобы разговор был за счёт вызываемого лица.

yah khah-CHOO, SHTOH-bï ruhz-gah-VOHR bïl zah-SHHOHT vï-zï-VAH-yih-muh-vuh l^yee-TSAH.

554. Please bill me at my home phone number.

Отнесите счёт на мой домашний номер телефона.

aht-n^yih-S^yEE-t^yih shhoht nah-MOY dah-MAHSH-n^yee NOH-m^yihr t^yih-l^yih-FOH-nuh.

555. They do not answer.

Не отвечают. *n^yih-aht-v^yih-CHAH-yoot.*

556. The line is busy.

Линия занята. *L^yEE-n^yee-yuh zuh-n^yih-TAH.*

557. Hello (on the telephone).

Алло (OR: Я вас слушаю).

ah-L^yOH (OR: yah vahs SLOO-shuh-yoo).

558. You have given me the wrong number.

Вы дали мне неправильный номер.

vï DAH-lʸee mnʸeh nʸih-PRAH-vʸeelʸ-nï__ee NOH-mʸihr.

559. This is [Victor] speaking.

Это [Виктор] говорит.

EH-tuh [VʸEEK-tuhr] guh-vah-RʸEET.

560. With whom do you want to speak?

С кем вы хотите говорить?

skʸehm vï khah-TʸEE-tʸih guh-vah-RʸEETʸ?

561. Hold the line (LIT.: Wait by the phone).

Подождите у телефона.

puh-dahzh-DʸEE-tʸih oo-tʸih-lʸih-FOH-nuh.

562. Dial again.

Наберите ещё раз.

nuh-bʸih-RʸEE-tʸih yih-SHHOH rahs.

563. I cannot hear you.

Не слышно. *nʸih-SLЫSH-nuh.*

564. The connection is poor.

Связь плохая. *svʸahsʸ plah-KHAH-yuh.*

565. Speak louder.

Говорите громче. *guh-vah-RʸEE-tʸih GROHM-chih.*

566. We have been cut off.

Нас разъединили. *nahs ruhz-yih-dʸee-NʸEE-lʸee.*

567. Call [him] [her] to the phone.

Попросите [его] [её] к телефону.

puh-prah-SʸEE-tʸih [yih-VOH] [yih-YOH] ktʸih-lʸih-FOH-noo.

568. [He] [She] is not here.

[Его] [Её] нет здесь.

[yih-VOH] [yih-YOH] nʸeht zdʸehsʸ.

569. You are wanted on the telephone.

Вас просят к телефону.

vahs PROH-s^yuht kt^yih-l^yih-FOH-noo.

570. May I leave a message?

Вы сможете передать то, что я скажу?

vï SMOH-zhuh-t^yih p^yih-r^yih-DAHT^y TOH-shtuh yah skah-ZHOO?

571. Call me back as soon as possible.

Перезвоните мне как можно скорее.

p^yih-r^yih-zvah-N^yEE-t^yih mn^yeh kahk MOHZH-nuh skah-R^yEH-yih.

572. I will call back later.

Я перезвоню позже.

yah p^yih-r^yih-zvah-N^yOO POH-zhhih.

573. I will wait for your call until [six] o'clock.

Я буду ждать вашего звонка до [шести] часов.

yah BOO-doo zhdaht^y VAH-shuh-vuh zvahn-KAH duh-[shï-ST^yEE] chih-SOHF.

HOTEL

574. I am looking for [a good hotel].

Я ищу [хорошую гостиницу].

yah ee-SHHOO [khah-ROH-shoo-yoo gah-ST^yEE-n^yee-tsoo].

575. —the best hotel.

—наилучшую гостиницу.

—nuh-ee-LOOCH-shoo-yoo gah-ST^yEE-n^yee-tsoo.

576. —an inexpensive hotel.

—недорогу́ю гости́ницу.

—*nʸih-duh-rah-GOO-yoo gah-ST ʸEE-nʸee-tsoo.*

577. I want to be in the center of town.

Я хочу́ бы́ть в це́нтре го́рода.

yah kha-CHOO bïtʸ FTSEHN-trʸih GOH-ruh-duh.

578. I want a quiet location.

Я хочу́ бы́ть в ти́хой ча́сти го́рода.

yah khah-CHOO bïtʸ FT ʸEE-khuh‿ee CHAHS-tʸee
GOH-ruh-duh.

579. I prefer to be close to [the university].

Я предпочита́ю бы́ть побли́же к [университе́ту].

yah prʸiht-puh-chih-TAH-yoo bïtʸ pah-BLʸEE-zhï
k[oo-nʸee-vʸihr-sʸee-T ʸEH-too].

580. I have a reservation for tonight.

Я заброни́ровал (F.: заброни́ровала) но́мер на
сего́дняшнюю но́чь.

yah zuh-brah-N ʸEE-ruh-vuhl (F.: zuh-brah-N ʸEE-ruh-
vuh-luh) NOH-mʸihr nuh-sʸih-VOHD-nʸish-nʸoo-yoo
nohch.

581. Where is the registration desk?

Где́ регистра́ция? *gdʸeh rʸih-gʸee-STRAH-tsï-yuh?*

582. Fill out this registration form.

Запо́лните э́ту фо́рму.

zah-POHL-nʸee-tʸih EH-too FOHR-moo.

583. Sign here, please.

Распиши́тесь здéсь, пожа́луйста.

ruhs-pʸee-SHÏ-tʸihsʸ zdʸehsʸ, pah-ZHAH-lï-stuh.

584. Leave your passport.

Остáвьте вáш пáспорт.

ah-STAHF ʸ-tʸih vahsh PAHS-puhrt.

585. You may pick it up later.
Вы смо́жете его́ забра́ть по́зже.
vï SMOH-zhuh-t^yih yih-VOH zah-BRAHT^y POH-zhhih.

586. Do you have [a single room]?
Есть у вас [но́мер на одного́]?
yehst^y oo-VAHS [NOH-m^yihr nah-ahd-nah-VOH]?

587. —a double room.
—но́мер на двои́х.   —*NOH-m^yihr nuh-dvah-YEEKH.*

588. —an air-conditioned room.
—но́мер с кондиционе́ром.
—*NOH-m^yihr skuhn-d^yee-tsï-ah-N^yEH-ruhm.*

589. —a suite.
—но́мер из не́скольких ко́мнат.
—*NOH-m^yihr eez-N^yEH-skuhl^y-k^yeekh KOHM-nuht.*

590. —a quiet room.
—ти́хий но́мер.   —*T^yEE-kh^yee NOH-m^yihr.*

591. —an inside room.
—но́мер с о́кнами на двор.
—*NOH-m^yihr SOHK-nuh-m^yee nah-DVOHR.*

592. —an outside room.
—но́мер с о́кнами на у́лицу.
—*NOH-m^yihr SOHK-nuh-m^yee nah-OO-l^yee-tsoo.*

593. —a room with a pretty view.
—но́мер с прия́тным ви́дом.
—*NOH-m^yihr spr^yee-YAHT-nïm V^yEE-duhm.*

594. I want a room [with a double bed].
Я хочу́ но́мер [с двуспа́льной крова́тью].
yah khah-CHOO NOH-m^yihr [zdvoo-SPAHL^y-nuh_ee krah-VAHT^y-yoo].

595. —with twin beds.
—с двумя́ крова́тями.
—*zdvoo-M*ᵞ*AH krah-VAH-t*ᵞ*ih-m*ᵞ*ee.*

596. —with a bath.
—с ва́нной.   —*SVAHN-nuh⌣ee.*

597. —with a shower.
—с ду́шем.   —*ZDOO-shuhm.*

598. —with running water.
—с водопрово́дом.   —*svuh-duh-prah-VOH-duhm.*

599. —with hot water.
—с горя́чей водо́й.   —*zgah-R*ᵞ*AH-chih⌣ee vah-DOY.*

600. —with a balcony.
—с балко́ном.   —*zbahl-KOH-nuhm.*

601. —with television.
—с телеви́зором.   —*st*ᵞ*ih-l*ᵞ*ih-V*ᵞ*EE-zuh-ruhm.*

602. I shall take a room [for one night].
Мне ну́жен но́мер [на одну́ но́чь].
*mn*ᵞ*eh NOO-zhuhn NOH-m*ᵞ*ihr [nah-ahd-NOO nohch].*

603. —for several days.
—на не́сколько дне́й.
—*nah-N*ᵞ*EH-skuhl*ᵞ*-kuh dn*ᵞ*eh⌣ee.*

604. —for a week or so.
—приблизи́тельно на неде́лю.
—*pr*ᵞ*ee-bl*ᵞ*ee-Z*ᵞ*EE-t*ᵞ*ihl*ᵞ*-nuh nuh-n*ᵞ*ih-D*ᵞ*EH-l*ᵞ*oo.*

605. Can I have it [with meals]?
Мо́жно снять его́ [с пита́нием]?
*MOHZH-nuh sn*ᵞ*aht*ᵞ *yih-VOH [sp*ᵞ*ee-TAH-n*ᵞ*ee-yihm]?*

606. —without meals.
—без пита́ния.   —*b*ᵞ*ihs-p*ᵞ*ee-TAH-n*ᵞ*ee-yuh.*

607. —with breakfast only.

—то́лько с за́втраком.

—*TOHL^y-kuh ZZAHF-truh-kuhm.*

608. What is the rate [per night]?

Ско́лько сто́ит но́мер [в су́тки]?

SKOHL^y-kuh STOH-yiht NOH-m^yihr [FSOOT-k^yee]?

609. —per week. —в неде́лю. —*vn^yih-D^yEH-l^yoo.*

610. —per month. —в ме́сяц. —*VM^yEH-s^yihts.*

611. Is service included?

Вхо́дит ли обслу́живание в сто́имость но́мера?

FKHOH-d^yiht-l^yee ahp-SLOO-zhï-vuh-n^yee-yuh FSTOH-ee-muhst^y NOH-m^yih-ruh?

612. I should like to see the room.

Я хоте́л (F.: хоте́ла) бы посмотре́ть но́мер.

yah khah-T^yEHL (F.: khah-T^yEH-luh)-bï puh-smah-TR^yEHT^y NOH-m^yihr.

613. Have you something [better]?

Éсть у ва́с но́мер [полу́чше]?

yehst^y oo-VAHS NOH-m^yihr [pah-LOOCH-shï]?

614. —cheaper. —подеше́вле. —*puh-d^yih-SHEHV-l^yih.*

615. —larger. —побо́льше. —*pah-BOHL^y-shï.*

616. —smaller. —поме́ньше. —*pah-M^yEHN^y-shï.*

617. —on a [lower] [higher] floor.

—где́-нибудь [пони́же] [повы́ше].

—*GD^yEH-n^yee-boot^y [pah-N^yEE-zhï] [pah-VÏ-shï].*

618. —with more light.

—посветле́е. —*pah-sv^yiht-L^yEH-yih.*

619. —with more air.

—ме́нее ду́шный. —*M^yEH-n^yih-yih DOOSH-nï_ee.*

620. —more attractively furnished.
—с мéбелью полýчше.
—*SM*ʸ*EH-b*ʸ*ihl*ʸ*-yoo pah-LOOCH-shï.*

621. —with a view of the sea.
—с вѝдом на мóре.　—*SV*ʸ*EE-duhm nah-MOH-r*ʸ*uh.*

622. It's too noisy.
Здéсь слѝшком шýмно.
*zd*ʸ*ehs*ʸ *SL*ʸ*EESH-kuhm SHOOM-nuh.*

623. This is satisfactory.
Э́тот нóмер вполнé хорóший.
*EH-tuht NOH-m*ʸ*ihr fpahl-N*ʸ*EH khah-ROH-shï＿ee.*

624. Is there [an elevator]?
Éсть ли [лифт]?　*YEHST*ʸ*-l*ʸ*ee [l*ʸ*eeft]?*

625. Upstairs. Наверхý. *nuh-v*ʸ*ihr-KHOO.*

626. Downstairs. Внизý. *vn*ʸ*ee-ZOO.*

627. What is my room number?
Какóй у меня́ нóмер?
*kah-KOY oo-m*ʸ*ih-N*ʸ*AH NOH-m*ʸ*ihr?*

628. Give me my room key.
Дáйте мнé ключ от моегó нóмера.
*DAH＿EE-t*ʸ*ih mn*ʸ*eh kl*ʸ*ooch aht-muh-yih-VOH NOH-m*ʸ*ih-ruh.*

629. [Take] [bring] my luggage upstairs.
[Отнесите] [принесите] мóй багáж навéрх.
*[aht-n*ʸ*ih-S*ʸ*EE-t*ʸ*ih] [pr*ʸ*ee-n*ʸ*ih-S*ʸ*EE-t*ʸ*ih] moy bah-GAHSH nah-V*ʸ*EHRKH.*

630. Tell the chambermaid to get my room ready.
Скажите, чтóбы гóрничная приготóвила мóй нóмер.
*skah-ZHÏ-t*ʸ*ih, SHTOH-bï GOHR-n*ʸ*eech-nuh-yuh pr*ʸ*ee-gah-TOH-v*ʸ*ee-luh moy NOH-m*ʸ*ihr.*

631. Wake me [at eight in the morning].

Разбуди́те меня́ [в во́семь часо́в утра́].

ruhz-boo-D^yEE-t^yih m^yih-N^YAH [VVOH-s^yihm^y
chih-SOHF oo-TRAH].

632. Do not disturb me until then.

Не беспоко́йте меня́ ра́ньше.

n^yih-b^yihs-pah-KOY-t^yih m^yih-N^YAH RAHN^Y-shï.

633. I want [breakfast] in my room.

Я хочу́ [за́втракать] у себя́ в но́мере.

yah khah-CHOO [ZAHF-truh-kuht^y] oo-s^yih-B^YAH
VNOH-m^yih-r^yih.

634. Room service, please.

Обслу́живание, пожа́луйста.

ahp-SLOO-zhï-vuh-n^yee-yuh, pah-ZHAH-lï-stuh.

635. Please bring me [some ice cubes].

Прошу́ принести́ [не́сколько ку́биков льда].

prah-SHOO pr^yee-n^yih-ST^YEE [N^YEH-skuhl^y-kuh
KOO-b^yee-kuhf l^ydah].

636. Do you have [a letter] for me?

Есть ли [письмо́] для меня́?

YEHST^y-l^yee [p^yees^y-MOH] dl^yuh-m^yih-N^YAH?

637. —a message. —запи́ска. —*zah-P^YEES-kuh.*

638. —a parcel. —посы́лка. —*pah-SÏL-kuh.*

639. Send [a chambermaid].

Вы́зовите [го́рничную].

VÏ-zuh-v^yee-t^yih GOHR-n^yeech-noo-yoo.

640. —[woman] [man] on floor duty.

—[дежу́рную] [дежу́рного] по коридо́ру.

—[d^yih-ZHOOR-noo-yoo] [d^yih-ZHOOR-nuh-vuh]
puh-kuh-r^yee-DOH-roo.

641. —a waiter.
—официа́нта. —*ah-f ʸee-tsï-AHN-tuh.*

642. —a porter.
—носи́льщика. —*nah-SʸEELʸ-shhee-kuh.*

643. I am expecting [a friend] [a guest].
Я ожида́ю [прия́теля (F.: прия́тельницу)] [го́стя].
yah ah-zhï-DAH-yoo [prʸee-YAH-tʸih-lʸuh
   (F.: *prʸee-YAH-tʸihlʸ-nʸee-tsoo)] [GOH-stʸuh].*

644. —a telephone call.
—звонка́. —*zvahn-KAH.*

645. Has anyone called?
Звони́л ли кто́-нибудь?
zvah-NʸEEL-lʸee KTOH-nʸee-bootʸ?

646. Send [him] [her] up.
Попроси́те [его́] [её] наве́рх.
puh-prah-SʸEE-tʸih [yih-VOH] [yih-YOH]
   nah-VʸEHRKH.

647. I shall not be here for lunch.
Я не бу́ду здесь обе́дать.
yah nʸih-BOO-doo zdʸehsʸ ah-BʸEH-dahtʸ.

648. May I leave [these valuables] in the hotel safe?
Мо́жно оста́вить [э́ти це́нности] в сейфе гости́ницы?
MOHZH-nuh ah-STAH-vʸeetʸ [EH-tʸee TSEHN-nuh-stʸee] FSʸEH ‿EE-fʸih gah-STʸEE-nʸee-tsï?

649. I would like to get [my things] from the safe.
Я хоте́л (F.: хоте́ла) бы взять [мои́ ве́щи] из сейфа.
yah khah-TʸEHL (F.: khah-TʸEH-luh)-bï vzʸahtʸ [mah-YEE VʸEH-shhee] ees-SʸEH ‿EE-fuh.

650. When must I check out?
Когда́ на́до освободи́ть но́мер?
kahg-DAH NAH-duh ah-svuh-bah-DʸEETʸ NOH-mʸihr?

651. I am leaving [at 10 o'clock].

Я уезжа́ю [в де́сять часо́в].

yah oo-yih-ZHHAH-yoo [VD^yEH-s^yiht^y chih-SOHF].

652. Make out my bill [as soon as possible].

Пригото́вьте мне́ счёт [ка́к мо́жно скоре́е].

pr^yee-gah-TOHF^y-t^yih mn^yeh shhoht [kahk MOHZH-nuh skah-R^yEH-yih].

653. The cashier.

Касси́р (F.: Касси́рша).

kahs-S^yEER (F.: kahs-S^yEER-shuh).

654. The doorman. Швейца́р. *shv^yih‿ee-TSAHR.*

655. The lobby. Вестибю́ль. *v^yih-st^yee-B^yOOL^y.*

656. Service Bureau (for ordering tickets, making travel arrangements, etc.).

Бюро́ обслу́живания.

b^yoo-ROH ahp-SLOO-zhï-vuh-n^yee-yuh.

CHAMBERMAID

657. The door doesn't lock.

Замо́к в двери́ не рабо́тает.

zah-MOHK vdv^yih-R^yEE n^yih-rah-BOH-tuh-yiht.

658. The [toilet] is broken.

[Туале́т] не рабо́тает.

[too-ah-L^yEHT] n^yih-rah-BOH-tuh-yiht.

659. The room is too [cold] [hot].

В но́мере сли́шком [хо́лодно] [жа́рко].

VNOH-m^yih-r^yih SL^yEESH-kuhm [KHOH-luhd-nuh] [ZHAHR-kuh].

660. There is no hot water.

Нет горячей воды.

n^{y}eht gah-R^{y}AH-chih＿ee vah-DÏ.

661. Spray [for insects].

Опрыскайте номер [от насекомых].

ah-PRÏS-kuh＿ee-t^{y}ih NOH-m^{y}ihr [aht-nuh-s^{y}ih-KOH-mĭkh].

662. —for vermin.

—от паразитов.   *—aht-puh-rah-Z^{y}EE-tuhf.*

663. Wash and iron [this shirt].

Выстирайте и погладьте [эту рубашку].

vï-st^{y}ee-RAH＿EE-t^{y}ih ee pah-GLAHT^y-t^{y}ih [EH-too roo-BAHSH-koo].

664. Bring me [another blanket].

Принесите мне [ещё одеяло].

pr^{y}ee-n^{y}ih-S^{y}EE-t^{y}ih mn^{y}eh [yih-SHHOH ah-d^{y}ih-YAH-luh].

665. Change the sheets.

Перемените простыни.

p^{y}ih-r^{y}ih-m^{y}ih-N^{y}EE-t^{y}ih PROH-stï-n^{y}ee.

666. Make the bed.

Приготовьте постель.

pr^{y}ee-gah-TOHF^y-t^{y}ih pah-ST^{y}EHL^y.

667. A bath mat.

Резиновый коврик.

r^{y}ih-Z^{y}EE-nuh-vï＿ee KOHV-r^{y}eek.

668. A bed sheet.   Простыня.   *pruh-stï-N^{y}AH.*

669. A candle.   Свечка.   *SV^{y}EHCH-kuh.*

670. Some coathangers.

Несколько вешалек.

N^{y}EH-skuhl^y-kuh V^{y}EH-shuh-l^{y}ihk.

671. A glass. Стака́н. *stah-KAHN.*

672. A pillow. Поду́шка. *pah-DOOSH-kuh.*

673. A pillowcase.
На́волочка. *NAH-vuh-luhch-kuh.*

674. An adapter for electrical appliances.
Ада́птер. *ah-DAHP-tʸihr.*

675. Some soap. Мы́ла. *MĬ-luh.*

676. Some toilet paper.
Туале́тной бума́ги.
too-ah-Lʸ EHT-nuh ̲ee boo-MAH-gʸee.

677. A towel. Полоте́нце. *puh-lah-Tʸ EHN-tsuh.*

678. A wash basin.
Умыва́льник. *oo-mĭ-VAHLʸ-nʸeek.*

679. A washcloth.*
Ма́ленькое полоте́нце для мытья́.
*MAH-lʸ ihnʸ-kuh-yuh puh-lah-Tʸ EHN-tsuh
dlʸ uh-mïtʸ-YAH.*

HOUSEKEEPING

680. Alarm clock.
Буди́льник. *boo-Dʸ EELʸ-nʸeek.*

681. Ashtray. Пе́пельница. *Pʸ EH-pʸ ihlʸ-nʸee-tsuh.*

682. Bathtub. Ва́нна. *VAHN-nuh.*

683. Bedroom. Спа́льня. *SPAHLʸ-nʸuh.*

684. Bottle opener. Што́пор. *SHTOH-puhr.*

---

* Instead of washcloths, Soviet hotels usually supply a fibrous scrubbing sponge (luffa) called моча́лка (*mah-CHAHL-kuh*).

685. Broom. Метла́. *mʸiht-LAH.*

686. Can opener.
Клю́ч для консе́рвов.
klʸooch dlʸuh-kahn-SʸEHR-vuhf.

687. Cat.
Ко́шка (OR: Ко́т). *KOHSH-kuh* (OR: *koht*).

688. Chair. Сту́л. *stool.*

689. Chest of drawers.
Комо́д (OR: Я́щики для белья́).
kah-MOHT (OR: *YAH-shhee-kʸee dlʸuh-bʸihlʸ-YAH*).

690. Clock. Часы́. *chih-SЇ.*

691. [Wall] closet.
[Стенно́й] шка́ф. *[stʸihn-NOY] shkahf.*

692. Cook.
По́вар (F.: Повари́ха).
POH-vuhr (F.: *puh-vah-RʸEE-khuh*).

693. Cork (stopper). Про́бка. *PROHP-kuh.*

694. Corkscrew. Што́пор. *SHTOH-puhr.*

695. Curtains. Занаве́ски. *zuh-nah-VʸEHS-kʸee.*

696. Cushion.
Дива́нная поду́шка.
dʸee-VAHN-nuh-yuh pah-DOOSH-kuh.

697. Dining room. Столо́вая. *stah-LOH-vuh-yuh.*

698. Dishes. Посу́да. *pah-SOO-duh.*

699. Dishwasher.
Автомати́ческая мо́йка (для посу́ды).
ahf-tuh-mah-TʸEE-chih-skuh-yuh MOY-kuh (dlʸuh-pah-SOO-dï).

700. Dog. Соба́ка. *sah-BAH-kuh.*

701. Doorbell.
Дверно́й звоно́к. *dv^yihr-NOY zvah-NOHK.*

702. Drapes. Драпиро́вка. *druh-p^yee-ROHF-kuh.*

703. Dryer. Суши́лка. *soo-SHĬL-kuh.*

704. Fan (electric/hand).
Вентиля́тор/Ве́ер. *v^yihn-t^yee-L^yAH-tuhr/V^yEH-yihr.*

705. Floor. По́л. *pohl.*

706. Hassock. Пу́фик. *POO-f^yeek.*

707. Kitchen. Ку́хня. *KOOKH-n^yuh.*

708. Lamp. Ла́мпа. *LAHM-puh.*

709. Light bulb. Ла́мпочка. *LAHM-puhch-kuh.*

710. Linens. Бельё. *b^yihl^y-YOH.*

711. Living room. Гости́ная. *gah-ST^yEE-nuh-yuh.*

712. Mosquito net (small net for face/large net).
Накома́рник/Противокома́рная се́тка.
nuh-kah-MAHR-n^yeek/pruh-t^yee-vuh-kah-MAHR-nuh-yuh S^yEHT-kuh.

713. Pail. (OR: **Bucket**).
Ведро́. *v^yih-DROH.*

714. Rug. Ковёр. *kah-V^yOHR.*

715. Sink. Ра́ковина. *RAH-kuh-v^yee-nuh.*

716. Switch (light).
Выключа́тель. *vï-kl^yoo-CHAH-t^yihl^y.*

717. Table. Сто́л. *stohl.*

718. Tablecloth. Ска́терть. *SKAH-t^yihrt^y.*

719. Terrace. Терра́са. *t^yih-RAH-suh.*

720. Tray. Подно́с. *pahd-NOHS.*

721. Vase. Ва́за. *VAH-zuh.*

722. Venetian blinds.
Подъёмные жалюзи́.
pahd-YOHM-nï-yih zhuh-l^yoo-Z^yEE.

723. Washing machine.
Стира́льная маши́на.
st^yee-RAHL^y-nuh-yuh mah-SHÏ-nuh.

724. Whiskbroom. Ве́ничек. *V^yEH-n^yee-chihk.*

725. Window shades. Што́рки. *SHTOHR-k^yee.*

CAFÉ AND BAR

726. Bartender, I'd like [a drink].
Ба́рмен, я хоте́л (F.: хоте́ла) бы [что́-нибудь вы́пить].
BAHR-mehn, yah khah-T^yEHL (F.: khah-T^yEH-luh)-bï [SHTOH-n^yee-boot^y VÏ-p^yeet^y].

727. —a cocktail. —кокте́йл. —*kahk-TEH_EEL.*

728. —a bottle of mineral water [without gas].
—буты́лку [негазиро́ванной] минера́льной воды́.
—*boo-TÏL-koo [n^yih-guh-z^yee-ROH-vuhn-nuh_ee] m^yee-n^yih-RAHL^y-nuh_ee vah-DÏ.*

729. —a whiskey [and soda].
—ви́ски [с со́довой].
—*V^yEE-sk^yee [SSOH-duh-vuh_ee].*

730. —a cognac. —конья́к. —*kahn^y-YANK.*

731. —a brandy. —бре́нди. —*BREHN-d^yee.*

732. —a liqueur. —ликёр. —*l^yee-K^yOHR.*

733. —a gin [and tonic].
—джи́н [с то́ником]. —*jïn [STOH-n^yee-kuhm].*

734. —rum. —ро́м. —*rohm.*

735. —Scotch whiskey.
—шотла́ндское ви́ски.
—*shaht-LAHNT-skuh-yuh V*ʸ*EE-sk*ʸ*ee.*

736. —rye whiskey.
—хле́бную во́дку. —*KHL*ʸ*EHB-noo-yoo VOHT-koo.*

737. —bourbon whiskey.
—бе́рбон. —*BEHR-buhn.*

738. —vermouth. —ве́рмут. —*V*ʸ*EHR-moot.*

739. —vodka. —во́дку. —*VOHT-koo.*

740. —a lemonade. —лимона́д. —*l*ʸ*ee-mah-NAHT.*

741. —a nonalcoholic drink.
—безалкого́льный напи́ток.
—*b*ʸ*ih-zuhl-kah-GOHL*ʸ*-nï‿ee nah-P*ʸ*EE-tuhk.*

742. —a bottled fruit drink.
—фрукто́вый напи́ток в буты́лке.
—*frook-TOH-vï‿ee nah-P*ʸ*EE-tuhk vboo-TÏL-k*ʸ*ih.*

743. —a bottle of [Pepsi-Cola].
—буты́лку [Пе́пси-ко́лы].
—*boo-TÏL-koo [PEHP-s*ʸ*ee-KOH-lï].*

744. —a light [draft] beer.
—све́тлое [бочко́вое] пи́во.
—*SV*ʸ*EHT-luh-yuh [bahch-KOH-vuh-yuh] P*ʸ*EE-vuh.*

745. —a dark beer.
—тёмное пи́во. —*T*ʸ*OHM-nuh-yuh P*ʸ*EE-vuh.*

746. —kvass (fermented drink made from black bread and malt).
—квас. —*kvahs.*

747. —[sweet] [semisweet] [semidry] [dry] champagne.

—[сла́дкое] [полусла́дкое] [полусухо́е] [сухо́е] шампа́нское.

—[*SLAHT-kuh-yuh*] [*puh-loo-SLAHT-kuh-yuh*] [*puh-loo-soo-KHOH-yuh*] [*soo-KHOH-yuh*] *shahm-PAHN-skuh-yuh.*

748. —a glass of [sherry] [port].

—рю́мку [хе́реса] [портве́йна].

—*RʸOOM-koo* [*KHEH-rʸih-suh*] [*pahrt-VʸEH＿EE-nuh*].

749. —[red] [white] [rosé] wine.

—[кра́сное] [бе́лое] [ро́зовое] вино́.

—[*KRAHS-nuh-yuh*] [*BʸEH-luh-yuh*] [*ROH-zuh-vuh-yuh*] *vʸee-NOH.*

750. Let's have another.

Вы́пьем ещё по одно́й.

VÏ-pʸyihm yih-SHHOH pah-ahd-NOY.

751. To your health!

За ва́ше здоро́вье! *zah-VAH-shuh zdah-ROHVʸ-yuh!*

RESTAURANT

752. Can you recommend a restaurant [for dinner (large midday meal)]?

Смо́жете ли вы́ рекомендова́ть рестора́н [для обе́да]?

SMOH-zhuh-tʸih-lʸee vï rʸih-kuh-mʸihn-dah-VAHTʸ rʸihs-tah-RAHN [dlʸuh-ah-BʸEH-duh]?

753. —for breakfast.

—для за́втрака. —*dlʸah-ZAHF-truh-kuh.*

754. —for a sandwich.

—для бутербро́да. —*dlʸuh-boo-tʸihr-BROH-duh.*

755. Do you serve [lunch]?
Подаёте ли вы [второй завтрак]?
puh-dah-YOH-t^yih-l^yee vï [ftah-ROY ZAHF-truhk]?

756. At what time is [supper] served?
В котором часу подают [ужин]?
fkah-TOH-ruhm chih-SOO puh-dah-YOOT [OO-zhïn]?

757. There are [three] of us.
Нас [трое].   *nahs [TROH-yuh].*

758. Are you my waiter? (LIT.: Are you serving this table?)
Вы обслуживаете этот стол?
vï ahp-SLOO-zhï-vuh-yih-t^yih EH-tuht stohl?

759. I prefer a table [by the window].
Я предпочитаю стол [у окна].
yah pr^yiht-puh-chee-TAH-yoo stohl [oo-ahk-NAH].

760. —in the corner. —в углу. —*voo-GLOO.*

761. —outdoors.
—на открытом воздухе.
—*nah-aht-KRÏ-tuhm VOHZ-doo-kh^yih.*

762. —indoors. —в зале. —*VZAH-l^yih.*

763. There is a draft here.
Здесь сквозняк (OR: Дует).
zd^yehs^y skvahz-N^yAHK (OR: DOO-yiht).

764. I'd like to wash my hands.
Я хотел (F.: хотела) бы помыть руки.
*yah khah-T^yEHL (F.: khah-T^yEH-luh)-bï pah-MÏT^y
ROO-k^yee.*

765. We want to dine [à la carte].
Мы хотим заказать [порционные блюда].
*mï khah-T^yEEM zuh-kah-ZAHT^y [puhr-tsï-OHN-nï-yih
BL^yOO-duh].*

766. —table d'hôte.

—дежу́рное блю́до.

—*d*ʸ*ih-ZHOOR-nuh-yuh BL*ʸ*OO-duh.*

767. We want to eat lightly.

Мы хоти́м закуси́ть.

*mï khah-T*ʸ*EEM zuh-koo-S*ʸ*EET*ʸ.

768. What is the specialty of the house?

Каки́е у ва́с фи́рменные блю́да?

*kah-K*ʸ*EE-yih oo-VAHS F*ʸ*EER-m*ʸ*ihn-nï-yih BL*ʸ*OO-duh?*

769. [What kind of fish] do you have?

[Кака́я] у ва́с [ры́ба]?

*[kah-KAH-yuh] oo-VAHS [R*Ï*-buh]?*

770. Please serve us as quickly as you can.

Принеси́те еду́, пожа́луйста, ка́к мо́жно скоре́е.

*pr*ʸ*ee-n*ʸ*ih-S*ʸ*EE-t*ʸ*ih yih-DOO, pah-ZHAH-lï-stuh, kahk MOHZH-nuh skah-R*ʸ*EH-yih.*

771. Call the wine steward.

Позови́те официа́нта с ка́ртой ви́н.

*puh-zah-V*ʸ*EE-t*ʸ*ih ah-f*ʸ*ee-tsï-AHN-tuh SKAHR-tuh_ee v*ʸ*een.*

772. Bring me [the menu].

Принеси́те мне́ [меню́].

*pr*ʸ*ee-n*ʸ*ih-S*ʸ*EE-t*ʸ*ih mn*ʸ*eh [m*ʸ*ih-N*ʸ*OO].*

773. —the wine list.

—ка́рту ви́н.   —*KAHR-too v*ʸ*een.*

774. —water [with ice] [without ice].

—воды́ [со льдо́м] [безо льда́].

—*vah-D*Ï *[sahl*ʸ*-DOHM] [b*ʸ*ih-zahl*ʸ*-DAH].*

775. —a napkin.   —салфе́тку.   —*sahl-F*ʸ*EHT-koo.*

776. —bread.   —хле́ба.   —*KHL*ʸ*EH-buh.*

777. —**butter.** —ма́сла. —*MAHS-luh.*

778. —**a cup.** —ча́шку. —*CHAHSH-koo.*

779. —**a fork.** —ви́лку. —*V^yEEL-koo.*

780. —**a [drinking glass] [wineglass] [shot glass].**
—[стака́н] [бока́л] [рю́мку].
—*[stah-KAHN] [bah-KAHL] [R^yOOM-koo].*

781. —**a [sharp] knife.**
—[о́стрый] нож. —*[OH-stri͜_ee] nohsh.*

782. —**a plate.** —таре́лку. —*tah-R^yEHL-koo.*

783. —**a large (OR: soup) spoon.**
—столо́вую ло́жку.
—*stah-LOH-voo-yoo LOHSH-koo.*

784. —**a saucer.** —блю́дце. —*BL^yOOT-tsuh.*

785. —**a teaspoon.**
—ча́йную ло́жку.
—*CHAH͜_EE-noo-yoo LOHSH-koo.*

786. **I want something [plain].**
Я хочу́ что́-нибудь [без припра́в].
yah khah-CHOO SHTOH-n^yee-boot^y [b^yihs-pr^yee-PRAHF].

787. —**without meat.**
—без мя́са. —*b^yihz-M^yAH-suh.*

788. **Is it [canned]?**
Это [консерви́рованное]?
EH-tuh [kuhn-s^yihr-V^yEE-ruh-vuhn-nuh-yuh]?

789. —**fatty (OR: greasy).**
—жи́рное. —*ZHÍR-nuh-yuh.*

790. —**fresh.** —свѐжее. —*SV^yEH-zhuh-yuh.*

791. —**frozen.**
—заморо́женное. —*zuh-mah-ROH-zhuhn-nuh-yuh.*

792. —lean —постное. —*POHS-nuh-yuh.*

793. —peppery.
—перченное. —*PʸEHR-chihn-nuh-yuh.*

794. —[very] salty.
—[очень] солёное. —*[OH-chihnʸ] sah-LʸOH-nuh-yuh.*

795. —spicy. —острое. —*OH-struh-yuh.*

796. —[very] sweet.
—[очень] сладкое. —*[OH-chihnʸ] SLAHT-kuh-yuh.*

797. How is it prepared?
Как приготовляют это блюдо?
kahk prʸee-guh-tahv-LʸAH-yoot EH-tuh BLʸOO-duh?

798. Is it [baked]?
Оно [печёное]? *ah-NOH [pʸih-CHOH-nuh-yuh]?*

799. —boiled. —варёное. —*vah-RʸOH-nuh-yuh.*

800. —braised.
—поджаренное в соку.
—*pahd-ZHAH-rʸihn-nuh-yuh fsah-KOO.*

801. —breaded.
—панированное. —*puh-nʸee-ROH-vuhn-nuh-yuh.*

802. —chopped.
—рубленное. —*ROO-blʸihn-nuh-yuh.*

803. —fried (OR: grilled).
—поджаренное. —*pahd-ZHAH-rʸihn-nuh-yuh.*

804. —ground. —молотое. —*MOH-luh-tuh-yuh.*

805. —roasted. —жареное. —*ZHAH-rʸih-nuh-yuh.*

806. on a skewer.
—на вертеле. —*nah-VʸEHR-tʸih-lʸih.*

807. This is [stale].
Это [чёрствое]. *EH-tuh CHOHR-stvuh-yuh.*

808. —too tough.
—сли́шком жёсткое.
—*SL'EESH-kuhm ZHOHST-kuh-yuh.*

809. —too dry.
—сли́шком сухо́е.   —*SL'EESH-kuhm soo-KHOH-yuh.*

810. I like the meat [rare].
Я хочу́ мя́со [с кро́вью].
yah khah-CHOO M'AH-suh [SKROHV'-yoo].

811. —medium.
—сре́дне поджа́ренное.
—*SR'EHD-n'ih pahd-ZHAH-r'ihn-nuh-yuh.*

812. —well done.
—прожа́ренное.   —*prah-ZHAH-r'ihn-nuh-yuh.*

813. This is [undercooked (OR: underboiled)].
Э́то [недожа́ренное (OR: недова́ренное)].
EH-tuh [n'ih-dah-ZHAH-r'ihn-nuh-yuh (OR: n'ih-dah-
VAH-r'ihn-nuh-yuh)].

814. —burned.
—пережа́ренное.   —*p'ih-r'ih-ZHAH-r'ihn-nuh-yuh.*

815. A little more.   Побо́льше.   *pah-BOHL'-shï.*

816. A little less.   Поме́ньше.   *pah-M'EHN'-shï.*

817. Something else.
Что́-нибудь друго́е.
SHTOH-n'ee-boot' droo-GOH-yuh.

818. A small portion.
Ма́ленькую по́рцию.
MAH-l'ihn'-koo-yoo POHR-tsï-yoo.

819. The next course.
Сле́дующее блю́до.
SL'EH-doo-yoo-shhuh-yuh BL'OO-duh.

820. I have had enough.

Мне хватит. *mnʸeh KHVAH-tʸiht.*

821. This is [not clean] [dirty].

Это [не чистое] [грязное].

EH-tuh [nʸih-CHEE-stuh-yuh] [GRʸAHZ-nuh-yuh].

822. This is too cold.

Это слишком холодное.

EH-tuh SLʸEESH-kuhm khah-LOHD-nuh-yuh.

823. I did not order this.

Я не заказывал (F.: не заказывала) этого.

yah nʸih-zah-KAH-zï-vuhl (F.: *nʸih-zah-KAH-zï-vuh-luh*)

EH-tuh-vuh.

824. You may take this away.

Можно это убрать.

MOHZH-nuh EH-tuh oo-BRAHTʸ.

825. May I change this for [a salad]?

Можно поменять это на [салат]?

MOHZH-nuh puh-mʸih-NʸAHTʸ EH-tuh nuh-

[*sah-LAHT*]?

826. What flavors do you have?

Какие у вас сорта?

kah-KʸEE-yih oo-VAHS sahr-TAH?

827. The check, please.

Дайте, пожалуйста, счёт.

DAH͜_EE-tʸih, pah-ZHAH-lï-stuh, shhoht.

828. Pay at the cashier's desk.

Заплатите, пожалуйста, в кассе.

zuh-plah-TʸEE-tʸih, pah-ZHAH-lï-stuh, FKAHS-sʸih.

829. Is the tip included?

Включены ли чаевые в счёт?

fklʸoo-chih-NÏ-lʸee chih-yih-VÏ-yih fshhoht?

830. There is a mistake in the bill.
В счёте ошибка. *FSHHOH-t^{y}ih ah-SHĬP-kuh.*

831. What are these charges for?
За что вы это посчитали?
zah-SHTOH vï EH-tuh puh-shhee-TAH-l^{y}ee?

832. The food and service were excellent.
Пища и обслуживание были прекрасны.
P^{y}EE-shhuh ee ahp-SLOO-zhï-vuh-n^{y}ee-yuh BĬ-l^{y}ee pr^{y}ih-KRAHS-nï.

833. Hearty appetite!
Приятного аппетита!
pr^{y}ee-YAHT-nuh-vuh ah-p^{y}ih-T^{y}EE-tuh!

834. Cloakroom.
Гардероб (OR: Раздевалка).
guhr-d^{y}ih-ROHP (OR: *ruhz-d^{y}ih-VAHL-kuh*).

835. Hatcheck number. Номерок. *nuh-m^{y}ih-ROHK.*

FOOD: SEASONINGS

(All items in the "Food" sections are alphabetized according to the Russian.)

836. [Hot] [mild] mustard.
[Острая] [неострая] горчица.
[*OH-struh-yuh*] [*n^{y}ih-OH-struh-yuh*] *gahr-CHEE-tsuh.*

837. Catsup. Кетчуп. *K^{y}EHT-choop.*

838. Fresh coriander. Кинзá. *k^{y}een-ZAH.*

839. Mayonnaise. Майонез. *muh-yah-NEHS.*

840. Oil. Масло. *MAHS-luh.*

841. Pepper. Перец. *P^{y}EH-r^{y}ihts.*

842. Gravy.
(Мясна́я) подли́вка.
(*m*ʸ*ihs-NAH-yuh*) *pahd-L*ʸ*EEF-kuh.*

843. Condiments. Припра́вы. *pr*ʸ*ee-PRAH-vï.*

844. Sugar. Са́хар. *SAH-khuhr.*

845. Salt. Со́ль. *sohl*ʸ.

846. Sauce. Со́ус. *soh⌣oos.*

847. Vinegar. У́ксус. *OOK-soos.*

848. Horseradish. Хре́н. *khr*ʸ*ehn.*

849. Garlic. Чесно́к. *chihs-NOHK.*

BEVERAGES

850. Hot chocolate.
Кака́о. *kah-KAH-oh.*

851. Kefir (a thin yoghurt drink).
Кефи́р. *k*ʸ*ih-F*ʸ*EER.*

852. [Black] coffee.
[Чёрный] ко́фе. *[CHOHR-nï⌣ee] KOH-f*ʸ*ih.*

853. Coffee with milk.
Ко́фе с молоко́м. *KOH-f*ʸ*ih smuh-lah-KOHM.*

854. Milk. Молоко́. *muh-lah-KOH.*

855. Milk shake.
Моло́чный кокте́йл.
muh-LOHCH-nï⌣ee kahk-TEH⌣EEL.

856. [Orange] [Grapefruit] juice.
[Апельси́новый] [Грейпфру́товый] со́к.
*[ah-p*ʸ*ihl*ʸ*-S*ʸ*EE-nuh-vï⌣ee] [gr*ʸ*ih⌣eep-FROO-tuh-
vï⌣ee] sohk.*

857. [Tomato] [Fruit] juice.
[Тома́тный] [Фрукто́вый] со́к.
[*tah-MAHT-nï͜ee*] [*frook-TOH-vï͜ee*] *sohk*.

858. Tea [with lemon] [with milk].
Ча́й [с лимо́ном] [с молоко́м].
chah͜ee [*sl*ᵞ*ee-MOH-nuhm*] [*smuh-lah-KOHM*].

859. Tea [with saccharine] [with cream].
Ча́й [с сахари́ном] [со сли́вками].
chah͜ee [*ssuh-khah-R*ᵞ*EE-nuhm*] [*sah-SL*ᵞ*EEF-kuh-m*ᵞ*ee*].

860. Iced [tea] [coffee].
[Ча́й] [ко́фе] со льдо́м.
[*chah͜ee*] [*KOH-f*ᵞ*ih*] *sahl*ᵞ*-DOHM*.

BREAKFAST FOODS

861. Pancakes (thin/extremely thin/thick).
Блины́/Бли́нчики/Ола́дьи.
*bl*ᵞ*ee-NÏ/BL*ᵞ*EEN-chee-k*ᵞ*ee/ah-LAHD*ᵞ*-yee*.

862. Rolls. Бу́лочки. *BOO-luhch-k*ᵞ*ee*.

863. Preserves. Варе́нье. *vah-R*ᵞ*EHN*ᵞ*-yuh*.

864. Jam. Дже́м. *jehm*.

865. [Buckwheat] [Wheat] [Rice] porridge.
[Гре́чневая] [Ма́нная] [Ри́совая] ка́ша.
[*GR*ᵞ*ECH-n*ᵞ*ih-vuh-yuh*] [*MAHN-nuh-yuh*]
  [*R*ᵞ*EE-suh-vuh-yuh*] *KAH-shuh*.

866. Marmalade. Мармела́д. *muhr-m*ᵞ*ih-LAHT*.

867. Oatmeal. Овся́нка. *ahf-S*ᵞ*AHN-kuh*.

868. Omelet [with mushrooms] [with cheese].
Омле́т [с гриба́ми] [с сы́ром].
*ahm-L*ᵞ*EHT* [*zgr*ᵞ*ee-BAH-m*ᵞ*ee*] [*SSÏ-ruhm*].

869. Pastry. Пиро́жное. *p^yee-ROHZH-nuh-yuh.*

870. Zwieback. Сухари́. *soo-khah-R^yEE.*

871. Toast.
Поджа́ренный хлеб. *pahd-ZHAH-r^yihn-nï‿ee khl^yehp.*

872. [Dark] [White] bread.
[Чёрный] [Бе́лый] хлеб.
[CHOHR-nï‿ee] [B^yEH-lï‿ee] khl^yehp.

873. [Scrambled] [Fried] eggs.
Яи́чница [болту́нья] [глазу́нья].
yih-YEESH-n^yee-tsuh [bahl-TOON^y-yuh]
  [glah-ZOON^y-yuh].

874. Poached eggs.
Яйца в мешо́чке.
YAH‿EE-tsuh vm^yih-SHOHCH-k^yih.

875. [Soft-boiled] [Hard-boiled] eggs.
Яйца [всмя́тку] [вкруту́ю].
YAH‿EE-tsuh [FSM^yAHT-koo] [fkroo-TOO-yoo].

876. Bacon and eggs.
Яйца с беко́ном. *YAH‿EE-tsuh zbeh-KOH-nuhm.*

MISCELLANEOUS
DAIRY PRODUCTS

877. Sheep cheese. Бры́нза. *BRÏN-zuh.*

878. Curd tarts. Ватру́шки. *vah-TROOSH-k^yee.*

879. Clabbered milk (similar to yoghurt).
Простоква́ша. *pruh-stah-KVAH-shuh.*

880. Baked yoghurt. Ря́женка. *R^yAH-zhuhn-kuh.*

881. [Mild] [Sharp] cheese.
[Неострый] [Острый] сыр.
[n^yih-OH-strï_ee] [OH-strï_ee] sïr.

882. Cheese fritters.
Сырники.   SÏR-n^yee-k^yee.

883. Sour cream. Сметана.   sm^yih-TAH-nuh.

884. Pot cheese. Творог.   tvah-ROHK.

APPETIZERS

885. Assorted [fish] [meat] plate.
Ассорти [рыбное] [мясное].
ah-sahr-T^yEE [RÏB-nuh-yuh] [m^yihs-NOH-yuh].

886. Eggplant "caviar."
Баклажанная икра.
buh-klah-ZHAHN-nuh-yuh ee-KRAH.

887. Cured fish fillet. Балык.   bah-LÏK.

888. Cold, boiled pork with garnish.
Буженина с гарниром.
boo-zhï-N^yEE-nuh zgahr-N^yEE-ruhm.

889. Salad with vegetables, eggs, meat, fish, and vinegar
dressing.
Винегрет.   v^yee-n^yih-GR^yEHT.

890. [Pickled] mushrooms.
[Маринованные] грибы.
[muh-r^yee-NOH-vuhn-nï-yih] gr^yee-BÏ.

891. [Red] [Black] caviar.
[Красная] [Чёрная] икра.
[KRAHS-nuh-yuh] [CHOHR-nuh-yuh] ee-KRAH.

892. [Pressed] [Unpressed] caviar.
[Па́юсная] [Зерни́стая] икра́.
[*PAH-yoos-nuh-yuh*] [*z'ihr-N'EE-stuh-yuh*] *ee-KRAH*.

893. [Beluga] [Russian sturgeon] [Sevruga] [Salmon] caviar.
[Белу́жья] [Осетро́вая] [Севрю́жья] [Ке́товая] икра́.
[*b'ih-LOOZH-yuh*] [*ah-s'ih-TROH-vuh-yuh*] [*s'ih-VR'OOZH-yuh*] [*K'EH-tuh-vuh-yuh*] *ee-KRAH*.

894. Sausage. Колбаса́. *kuhl-bah-SAH*.

895. Liver pâté.
Паштет из печёнки.
pahsh-T'EHT ees-p'ih-CHOHN-k'ee.

896. Meat-filled dumplings.
Пельме́ни. *p'ihl'-M'EH-n'ee*.

897. Piroshki (small pies) with [meat] [cabbage] [rice] [potatoes].
Пирожки́ с [мя́сом] [капу́стой] [ри́сом] [карто́шкой].
p'ee-rahsh-K'EE s[M'AH-suhm] [*kah-POO-stuh ee*] [*R'EE-suhm*] [*kahr-TOHSH-kuh ee*].

898. Fish in aspic.
Ры́бное заливно́е. *RĬB-nuh-yuh zuh-l'eev-NOH-yuh*.

899. Small sausages. Сарде́льки. *sahr-D'EHL'-k'ee*.

900. [Smoked] [Pickled] herring.
[Копчёная] [Марино́ванная] селёдка (OR: се́льдь).
[*kahp-CHOH-nuh-yuh*] [*muh-r'ee-NOH-vuhn-nuh-yuh*] *s'ih-L'OHT-kuh* (OR: *s'ehl't'*).

901. Smoked salmon. Сёмга. *S'OHM-guh*.

902. Wieners. Соси́ски. *sah-S'EES-k'ee*.

903. Jellied meat or fish.
Сту́день (OR: Холоде́ц).
STOO-d'ihn' (OR: *khuh-lah-D'EHTS*).

904. Fish-meat loaf appetizer.
Форшма́к. *fahr-SHMAHK.*

905. Sprats. Шпро́ты. *SHPROH-tï.*

SOUPS

906. [Beef] broth.
[Говя́жий] бульо́н. *[gah-V*^{y}*AH-zhï_ee] bool*^{y}*-YOHN.*

907. Borscht (beet and cabbage soup). Борщ. *bohrshh.*

908. Consommé.
Консоме́ (OR: Мясно́й бульо́н).
kohn-soh-MEH (OR: m^y*ihs-NOY bool*^{y}*-YOHN).*

909. Okroshka (cold vegetable soup with kvass and meat or fish).
Окро́шка. *ah-KROHSH-kuh.*

910. Rassolnik (tart sorrel soup with kidneys).
Рассо́льник. *rah-SOHL*^{y}*-n*^{y}*eek.*

911. [Meat] [Fish] solyanka (beef or fish soup with piquant vegetables).
Соля́нка [мясна́я] [ры́бная].
sah-L^y*AHN-kuh [m*^{y}*ihs-NAH-yuh] [RÏB-nuh-yuh].*

912. [Tomato] [Noodle] soup.
Су́п [из помидо́ров] [с лапшо́й].
soop [ees-puh-m^y*ee-DOH-ruhf] [slahp-SHOY].*

913. [Pea] [Mushroom] soup.
[Горо́ховый] [Грибно́й] су́п.
[gah-ROH-khuh-vï_ee] [gr^y*eeb-NOY] soop.*

914. [Chicken] [Vegetable] soup.
[Кури́ный] [Овощно́й] су́п.
[koo-R^y*EE-nï_ee] [ah-vahsh-NOY] soop.*

915. Cold beet soup.
Свекóльник. *sv^yih-KOHL^y-n^yeek.*

916. Chowder. Ухá. *oo-KHAH.*

917. Kharcho (spicy Georgian mutton soup).
Харчó. *khahr-CHOH.*

918. Cabbage soup. Щи́. *shhee.*

919. Schav (thick soup made of sorrel or spinach and soup greens).
Щи́ зелёные. *shhee z^yih-L^yOH-n ̈i-yih.*

SALADS

920. [Green] [Potato] salad.
[Зелёный] [Картóфельный] салáт.
[z^yih-L^yOH-n ̈i⌣ee] [kahr-TOH-f^yihl^yn ̈i⌣ee] sah-LAHT.

921. Seafood salad.
Ры́бный салáт. *RĪB-n ̈i⌣ee sah-LAHT.*

922. [Shrimp] [Chicken] salad.
Салáт [из кревéток] [из ку́р].
sah-LAHT [ees-kr^yih-V^yEH-tuhk] [ees-KOOR].

923. Tomato salad.
Салáт из помидóров.
sah-LAHT ees-puh-m^yee-DOH-ruhf.

924. Tart chicken or meat salad with sour-cream dressing.
Салáт Оливьé. *sah-LAHT ah-l^yeev^y-YEH.*

925. Salad dressing.
Сóус для салáта. *soh⌣oos dl^yuh-sah-LAH-tuh.*

926. Meat salad.
Столи́чный (OR: Мяснóй) салáт.
stah-L^yEECH-n ̈i⌣ee (OR: m^yihs-NOY) sah-LAHT.

MEATS

927. Mutton. Бара́нина. *bah-RAH-n^yee-nuh.*

928. Lamb.
Молода́я бара́нина.
muh-lah-DAH-yuh bah-RAH-n^yee-nuh.

929. Beef Stroganoff.
Бёф-стро́ганов. *b^yehf-STROH-guh-nuhf.*

930. Steak (steak/small thin steak/entrecôte/filet).
Бифште́кс/Лангéт/Антреко́т/Филé.
*b^yeef-SHTEHKS/lahn-G^yEHT/ahn-tr^yih-KOHT/
    f^yee-L^yEH.*

931. Ground beef.
Бифште́кс ру́бленный.
b^yeef-SHTEHKS ROO-bl^yihn-nï_ee.

932. Ham. Ветчина́. *v^yiht-chih-NAH.*

933. Beef. Говя́дина. *gah-V^yAH-d^yee-nuh.*

934. Goulash. Гуля́ш. *goo-L^yAHSH.*

935. Game. Дичь. *d^yeech.*

936. Spicy pot roast. Жарко́е. *zhahr-KOH-yuh.*

937. Wild boar. Каба́н. *kah-BAHN.*

938. Cutlets. Котлéты. *kaht-L^yEH-tï.*

939. Kulebyaka (meat or fish pie).
Кулебя́ка. *koo-l^yih-B^yAH-kuh.*

940. Ground lamb shish kebab.
Люля́-кеба́б. *l^yoo-L^yAH-k^yih-BAHP.*

941. Bear meat.
Медвежа́тина. *m^yihd-v^yih-ZHAH-t^yee-nuh.*

942. Brains. Мозги́. *mah-ZG^yEE.*

943. Venison. Олéнина. *ah-L^yEH-n^yee-nuh.*

944. Chops.
Отбивны́е котле́ты. *ahd-b^{y}eev-NĬ-yih kaht-L^{y}EH-tï.*

945. Liver. Печёнка. *p^{y}ih-CHOHN-kuh.*

946. Roast suckling pig with buckwheat kasha.
Поросёнок с ка́шей.
puh-rah-S^{y}OH-nuhk SKAH-shuh⌣ee.

947. Kidneys [in Madeira sauce].
По́чки [в маде́ре]. *POHCH-k^{y}ee [vmah-D^{y}EH-r^{y}ih].*

948. Stew. Рагу́. *rah-GOO.*

949. Roast beef. Ростби́ф. *rohz-B^{y}EEF.*

950. Meat loaf.
Мясно́й руле́т. *m^{y}ihs-NOY roo-L^{y}EHT.*

951. Pork. Свини́на. *sv^{y}ee-N^{y}EE-nuh.*

952. Heart. Се́рдце. *S^{y}EHR-tsuh.*

953. Veal. Теля́тина. *t^{y}ih-L^{y}AH-t^{y}ee-nuh.*

954. Meat balls (main course/in soup).
Мясны́е тефте́ли/Фрикаде́льки.
m^{y}ihs-NĬ-yih t^{y}ihf-T^{y}EH-l^{y}ee/fr^{y}ee-kah-D^{y}EHL^y-k^{y}ee.

955. Shish kebab. Шашлы́к. *shahsh-LĬK.*

POULTRY

956. Pigeon. Го́лубь. *GOH-loop^y.*

957. Goose. Гу́сь. *goos^y.*

958. Turkey. Инде́йка. *een-D^{y}EH⌣EE-kuh.*

959. Chicken Kiev.
Котле́ты по-ки́евски.
kaht-L^{y}EH-tï pah-K^{y}EE-yihf-sk^{y}ee.

960. Chicken cutlets.
Пожа́рские котле́ты.
pah-ZHAHR-sk^yee-yih kaht-L^yEH-tï.

961. Partridge. Куропа́тка. *koo-rah-PAHT-kuh.*

962. Chicken. Ку́ры. *KOO-rï.*

963. Hazel grouse. Ря́бчик. *R^yAHP-cheek.*

964. Duck. У́тка. *OOT-kuh.*

965. Chicken tabaka (whole small chicken, pressed and quick-fried).
Цыплёнок (PL.: Цыпля́та) табака́.
tsï-PL^yOH-nuhk (PL.: tsï-PL^yAH-tuh) tuh-bah-KAH.

FISH AND SEAFOOD

966. Beluga sturgeon (OR: White sturgeon).
Белу́га. *b^yih-LOO-guh.*

967. Sole. Ка́мбала. *KAHM-buh-luh.*

968. Crab. Кра́б. *krahp.*

969. Shrimp. Креве́тки. *kr^yih-V^yEHT-k^yee.*

970. Salmon. Лососи́на. *luh-sah-S^yEE-nuh.*

971. Swordfish. Ме́ч-ры́ба. *M^yEHCH-RÏ-buh.*

972. Burbot (type of freshwater cod).
Нали́м. *nah-L^yEEM.*

973. Bass. О́кунь. *OH-koon^y.*

974. Lobster. Ома́р. *ah-MAHR.*

975. Sturgeon. Осетри́на. *ah-s^yih-TR^yEE-nuh.*

976. Halibut. Па́лтус. *PAHL-toos.*

977. Crayfish. Ра́к. *rahk.*

978. Mussels.
Двуство́рчатые раку́шки.
dvoo-STVOHR-chih-tï-yih rah-KOOSH-k^{y}ee.

979. Sardines. Сарди́ны. *sahr-D^{y}EE-nï.*

980. Stellate sturgeon. Севрю́га. *s^{y}ihv-R^{y}OO-guh.*

981. Sheatfish (type of catfish). Сóм. *sohm.*

982. Sterlet (small sturgeon).
Стéрлядь. *ST^{y}EHR-l^{y}iht^y.*

983. Zander (OR: **Pike perch**). Суда́к. *soo-DAHK.*

984. Cod. Треска́. *tr^{y}ih-SKAH.*

985. Tuna. Тунéц. *too-N^{y}EHTS.*

986. Oysters. У́стрицы. *OO-str^{y}ee-tsï.*

987. Trout. Форéль. *fah-R^{y}EHL^y.*

988. Pike. Щу́ка. *SHHOO-kuh.*

VEGETABLES AND STARCHES

989. Artichokes.
Артишóки. *ahr-t^{y}ee-SHOH-k^{y}ee.*

990. Eggplant. Баклажáн. *buh-klah-ZHAHN.*

991. Beans. Бобы́. *bah-BÏ.*

992. Stuffed cabbage.
Голубцы́. *guh-loop-TSÏ.*

993. Peas. Горóшек. *gah-ROH-shuhk.*

994. Mushrooms. Грибы́. *gr^{y}ee-BÏ.*

995. Cabbage. Капу́ста. *kah-POO-stuh.*

996. Cauliflower.
Цветна́я капу́ста.
tsv^{y}iht-NAH-yuh kah-POO-stuh.

997. Potatoes. Картофель. *kahr-TOH-f^{y}ihl^y.*

998. Mashed potatoes.
Картофельное пюре.
kahr-TOH-f^{y}ihl^{y}nuh-yuh p^{y}oo-REH.

999. [Fried] [Boiled] potatoes.
[Жареный] [Отварной] картофель.
[ZHAH-r^{y}ih-ni‿ee] [aht-vahr-NOY] kahr-TOH-f^{y}ihl^y.

1000. [Baked] [Stuffed] potatoes.
[Печёный] [Фаршированный] картофель.
[p^{y}ih-CHOH-ni‿ee] [fuhr-shï-ROH-vuhn-ni‿ee]
kahr-TOH-f^{y}ihl^y.

1001. Kasha (buckwheat groats).
(Гречневая) каша.
(GR^{y}EHCH-n^{y}ih-vuh-yuh) KAH-shuh.

1002. Dumplings (plain/filled).
Клёцки/Вареники.
KL^{y}OHTS-k^{y}ee/vah-R^{y}EH-n^{y}ee-k^{y}ee.

1003. Noodles (flat, long/short).
Лапша/Лапша-ракушки.
lahp-SHAH/lahp-SHAH–rah-KOOSH-k^{y}ee.

1004. Onions. Лук. *look.*

1005. Macaroni. Макароны. *muh-kah-ROH-nï.*

1006. Carrots. Морковь. *mahr-KOHF^y.*

1007. Cucumbers. Огурцы. *ah-goor-TSÏ.*

1008. Pickles.
Солёные огурцы. *sah-L^{y}OH-nï-yih ah-goor-TSÏ.*

1009. Olives (green/black).
Оливки/Маслины. *ah-L^{y}EEF-k^{y}ee/mahs-L^{y}EE-nï.*

1010. Green peppers.
Зелёный перец. *z^{y}ih-L^{y}OH-nï‿ee P^{y}EH-r^{y}ihts.*

1011. Parsley. Петру́шка. *p^{y}ih-TROOSH-kuh.*

1012. Rice pilaf. Пло́в. *plohf.*

1013. Tomatoes. Помидо́ры. *puh-m^{y}ee-DOH-rï.*

1014. Rice. Рис. *r^{y}ees.*

1015. Lettuce.
Сала́т (OR: Ли́стья зелёного сала́та).
*sah-LAHT (OR: L^{y}EEST^y-yuh z^{y}ih-L^{y}OH-nuh-vuh
sah-LAH-tuh).*

1016. Celery. Сельдере́й. *s^{y}ihl^y-d^{y}ih-R^{y}EH‿EE.*

1017. Asparagus. Спа́ржа. *SPAHR-zhuh.*

1018. Wax (OR: **Yellow**) **beans.**
Жёлтая фасо́ль. *ZHOHL-tuh-yuh fah-SOHL^y.*

1019. Lima beans.
Ли́мская фасо́ль. *LEEM-skuh-yuh fah-SOHL^y.*

1020. Green beans.
Стручко́вая фасо́ль.
strooch-KOH-vuh-yuh fah-SOHL^y.

1021. Spinach. Шпина́т. *shp^{y}ee-NAHT.*

FRUITS

1022. Apricot. Абрико́с. *ah-br^{y}ee-KOHS.*

1023. Pineapple. Анана́с. *ah-nah-NAHS.*

1024. Orange. Апельси́н. *ah-p^{y}ihl^y-S^{y}EEN.*

1025. Watermelon. Арбу́з. *ahr-BOOS.*

1026. Apple charlotte.
Ба́бка я́блочная. *BAHP-kuh YAH-bluhch-nuh-yuh.*

1027. Banana. Бана́н. *bah-NAHN.*

1028. Grapes. Виногра́д. *v^{y}ee-nah-GRAHT.*

1029. Cherries (tart/sweet).
Ви́шня/Чере́шня. *V^yEESH-n^yuh/chih-R^yEHSH-n^yuh.*

1030. [A half] grapefruit.
[Полови́на] гре́йпфрута.
[puh-lah-V^yEE-nuh] GR^yEH ⎽EEP-froo-tuh.

1031. Pear. Гру́ша. *GROO-shuh.*

1032. Melon. Ды́ня. *DĬ-n^yuh.*

1033. Blackberries.
Ежеви́ка. *yih-zhĭ-V^yEE-kuh.*

1034. Figs. Инжи́р. *een-ZHĬR.*

1035. Cantaloupe. Кантапу́па. *kuhn-tah-LOO-puh.*

1036. Tart fruit purée. Кисе́ль. *k^yee-S^yEHL^y.*

1037. Strawberries (large/small, wild).
Клубни́ка/Земляни́ка.
kloob-N^yEE-kuh/z^yihm-l^yih-N^yEE-kuh.

1038. Cranberries. Клю́ква. *KL^yOOK-vuh.*

1039. Compote. Компо́т. *kahm-POHT.*

1040. Lemon. Лимо́н. *l^yee-MOHN.*

1041. Raspberries. Мали́на. *mah-L^yEE-nuh.*

1042. Tangerine. Мандари́н. *muhn-dah-R^yEEN.*

1043. Peach. Пе́рсик. *P^yEHR-s^yeek.*

1044. Plums. Сли́вы. *SL^yEE-vĭ.*

1045. Currants. Сморо́дина. *smah-ROH-d^yee-nuh.*

1046. Dates. Фи́ники. *F^yEE-n^yee-k^yee.*

1047. Blueberries. Черни́ка. *chihr-N^yEE-kuh.*

1048. Prunes. Черносли́в. *chihr-nah-SL^yEEF.*

1049. Apple. Я́блоко. *YAH-bluh-kuh.*

DESSERTS

1050. Dumplings filled with cheese or fruit.
Варе́ники. *vah-R^yEH-n^yee-k^yee.*

1051. Baked pudding.*
Запека́нка. *zuh-p^yih-KAHN-kuh.*

1052. Custard.
Заварно́й крем. *zuh-vahr-NOY kr^yehm.*

1053. [Vanilla] [Chocolate] [Creamy] ice cream.
[Вани́льное] [Шокола́дное] [Сли́вочное] моро́женое.
[vah-N^yEEL^y-nuh-yuh] [shuh-kah-LAHD-nuh-yuh]
[SL^yEE-vuhch-nuh-yuh] mah-ROH-zhuh-nuh-yuh.

1054. Napoleon. Наполео́н. *nuh-puh-l^yih-OHN.*

1055. Cookies. Пече́нье. *p^yih-CHEHN^y-yuh.*

1056. Pie (refers to both entrée and dessert pies).
Пиро́г. *p^yee-ROHK.*

1057. Extra-rich ice cream.
Пломби́р. *plahm-B^yEER.*

1058. Filled pastry. По́нчик. *POHN-cheek.*

1059. Pudding. Пу́динг. *POO-d^yeenk.*

1060. Cake (layer/loaf).
То́рт/Ке́кс. *tohrt/k^yehks.*

1061. Sherbet (chilled, sweetened fruit).
Шербе́т. *shïr-B^yEHT.*

1062. Eclair. Экле́р. *eh-KLEHR.*

---

* Made of kasha, cheese, meat or carrots—often serves as a
vegetable or starch. The version with cheese is sometimes served
with sugar for dessert.

SIGHTSEEING

1063. I want a licensed guide [who speaks English].
Я хочу профессионáльного гида [котóрый говорит
по-английски].
*yah khah-CHOO pruh-f^{y}ih-s^{y}ee-ah-NAHL^y-nuh-vuh
G^{y}EE-duh [kah-TOH-rï⁀ee guh-vah-R^{y}EET
pah-ahn-GL^{y}EE-sk^{y}ee].*

1064. How long will the excursion take?
Скóлько врéмени займёт экскýрсия?
*SKOHL^y-kuh VR^{y}EH-m^{y}ih-n^{y}ee zah⁀ee-M^{y}OHT
ehk-SKOOR-s^{y}ee-yuh?*

1065. Do I have to book in advance?
Нýжно зарáнее заказáть билéты?
*NOOZH-nuh zah-RAH-n^{y}ih-yih zuh-kah-ZAHT^y
b^{y}ee-L^{y}EH-tï?*

1066. Are admission tickets and a snack included?
Включены́ входны́е билéты и закýски?
*fkl^{y}oo-chih-N$\ddot{I}$ fkhahd-N$\ddot{I}$-yih b^{y}ee-L^{y}EH-tï ee
zah-KOOS-k^{y}ee?*

1067. What is the charge for a trip [to the island]?
Скóлько стóит поéздка [на óстров]?
*SKOHL^y-kuh STOH-yiht pah-YEHST-kuh
[nah-OH-struhf]?*

1068. —to the mountain.
—на гóру.   —*nah-GOH-roo.*

1069. —to the sea.   —на мóре.   —*nah-MOH-r^{y}uh.*

1070. —around the city.
—по гóроду.   —*pah-GOH-ruh-doo.*

1071. Call for me [tomorrow] at my hotel at 8 A.M.
Зайди́те за мной [за́втра] в гости́ницу в во́семь часо́в
    утра́.
zah‿ee-DᵞEE-tᵞih zah-MNOY [ZAHF-truh] vgahs-
    TᵞEE-nᵞee-tsoo VVOH-sᵞihmᵞ chih-SOHF oo-TRAH.

1072. Show me the sights of interest.
Покажи́те мне достопримеча́тельности.
puh-kah-ZHĬ-tᵞih mnᵞeh duh-stuh-prᵞee-mᵞih-CHAH-
    tᵞihlᵞ-nuh-stᵞee.

1073. What is that building?
Что в э́том зда́нии?   *shtoh VEH-tuhm ZDAH-nᵞee-yee?*

1074. How old is it?
Когда́ оно́ бы́ло постро́ено?
kahg-DAH ah-NOH BĬ-luh pah-STROH-yih-nuh?

1075. Can we go in?
Мо́жно войти́?   *MOHZH-nuh vah‿ee-TᵞEE?*

1076. I am interested in [architecture].
Я интересу́юсь [архитекту́рой].
yah een-tᵞih-rᵞih-SOO-yoosᵞ [ahr-khᵞee-tᵞihk-TOO-
    ruh‿ee].

1077. —archeology.
—археоло́гией.   *—ahr-khᵞih-ah-LOH-gᵞee-yih‿ee.*

1078. —sculpture.
—скульпту́рой.   *—skoolᵞp-TOO-ruh‿ee.*

1079. —painting.
—жи́вописью.   *—ZHĬ-vuh-pᵞeesᵞ-yoo.*

1080. —folk arts [and crafts].
—наро́дным тво́рчеством [и ремёслами].
—nah-ROHD-nïm TVOHR-chih-stvuhm [ee rᵞih-
    MᵞOHS-luh-mᵞee].

1081. —modern art.

—совреме́нным иску́сством.

—suh-vr^yih-M^yEHN-nïm ee-SKOO-stvuhm.

1082. I should like to see [the park].

Я хоте́л (F.: хоте́ла) бы посмотре́ть [па́рк].

yah khah-T^yEHL (F.: khah-T^yEH-luh)-bï puh-smah-TR^yEHT^y [pahrk].

1083. —the cathedral.

—собо́р (OR: хра́м).   *—sah-BOHR (OR: khrahm).*

1084. —the countryside (LIT.: nature).

—приро́ду.   *—pr^yee-ROH-doo.*

1085. —the library.

—библиоте́ку.   *—b^yee-bl^yee-ah-T^yEH-koo.*

1086. —the ruins.   —руи́ны.   *—roo-EE-nï.*

1087. —the castle.   —за́мок.   *—ZAH-muhk.*

1088. —the palace.   —дворе́ц.   *—dvah-R^yEHTS.*

1089. —the zoo.   —зоопа́рк.   *—zah-ah-PAHRK.*

1090. Let's take a walk around [the botanical garden].

Дава́йте похо́дим по [ботани́чискому са́ду].

dah-VAH‿EE-t^yih pah-KHOH-d^yeem puh-[buh-tah-N^yEE-chih-skuh-moo SAH-doo].

1091. A beautiful view!

Прекра́сный ви́д!   *pr^yih-KRAHS-nï‿ee v^yeet!*

1092. Very interesting!

О́чень интере́сно!   *OH-chihn^y een-t^yih-R^yEHS-nuh!*

1093. Magnificent!

Прекра́сно!   *pr^yih-KRAHS-nuh!*

1094. We are enjoying ourselves.

Мы́ хорошо́ прово́дим вре́мя.

mï khuh-rah-SHOH prah-VOH-d^yeem VR^yEH-m^yuh.

1095. I am bored. Мне́ ску́чно. *mn^yeh SKOOSH-nuh.*

1096. When does the museum [open] [close]?
Когда́ музе́й [открыва́ется] [закрыва́ется]?
*kahg-DAH moo-Z^yEH＿EE [aht-krï-VAH-yiht-tsuh]
[zuh-krï-VAH-yiht-tsuh]?*

1097. Is this the way [to the entrance]?
Сюда́ [ко вхо́ду]? *s^yoo-DAH [kahf-KHOH-doo]?*

1098. —to the exit. —к вы́ходу. —*KVÏ-khuh-doo.*

1099. Let's visit [the fine arts gallery].
Посети́м [галлере́ю изобрази́тельных иску́сств].
puh-s^yih-T^yEEM [guh-l^yih-R^yEH-yoo ee-zuh-brah-Z^yEE-t^yihl^y-nïkh ee-SKOOSTF].

1100. Let's stay longer.
Побу́дем до́льше. *pah-BOO-d^yihm DOHL^y-shï.*

1101. Let's leave now.
Уйдёмте сейча́с. *oo＿ee-D^yOHM-t^yih s^yih-CHAHS.*

1102. We must be back by 5 o'clock.
Мы должны́ верну́ться к пяти́ часа́м.
mï dahlzh-NÏ v^yihr-NOOT-tsuh kp^yih-T^yEE chih-SAHM.

1103. If there is time, let's rest a while.
Éсли бу́дет вре́мя, дава́йте немно́го отдохнём.
YEHS-l^yee BOO-d^yiht VR^yEH-m^yuh, dah-VAH＿EE-t^yih n^yihm-NOH-guh ahd-dahkh-N^yOHM.

WORSHIP

1104. Altar. Алта́рь. *ahl-TAHR^y.*

1105. Catholic church.
Католи́ческая це́рковь.
kuh-tah-L^yEE-chih-skuh-yuh TSEHR-kuhf^y.

1106. Choral music.
Хоровáя мýзыка. *khuh-rah-VAH-yuh MOO-zï-kuh.*

1107. Collection plate.
Тарéлка для сбóра дéнежных пожéртвований.
*tah-R^yEHL-kuh dl^yah-ZBOH-ruh D^yEH-n^yihzh-nïkh
pah-ZHEHRT-vuh-vuh-n^yee.*

1108. Communion.
Причáстие. *pr^yee-CHAH-st^yee-yuh.*

1109. Confession. Úсповедь. *EES-puh-v^yiht^y.*

1110. Contribution.
(Дéнежное) пожéртвование.
(D^yEH-n^yihzh-nuh-yuh) pah-ZHEHRT-vuh-vuh-n^yee-yuh.

1111. Mass (Orthodox/non-Orthodox).
Обéдня/Мéсса. *ah-B^yEHD-n^yuh/M^yES-suh.*

1112. Minister. Свящéнник. *sv^yih-SHHEHN-n^yeek.*

1113. Mosque. Мечéть. *m^yih-CHEHT^y.*

1114. Prayers. Молúтвы. *mah-L^yEET-vï.*

1115. Prayer book.
Молúтвенник. *mah-L^yEET-v^yihn-n^yeek.*

1116. Priest. Свящéнник. *sv^yih-SHHEHN-n^yeek.*

1117. Protestant church.
Протестáнтская цéрковь.
pruh-t^yih-STAHNT-skuh-yuh [TSEHR-kuhf^y.

1118. Rabbi. Раввúн. *rah-V^yEEN.*

1119. Religious school.
Религиóзная шкóла.
r^yih-l^yee-g^yee-OHZ-nuh-yuh SHKOH-luh.

1120. Synagogue. Синагóга. *s^yee-nah-GOH-guh.*

1121. Sermon. Прóповедь. *PROH-puh-v^yiht^y.*

1122. Services. Слýжба. *SLOOZH-buh.*

ENTERTAINMENTS

1123. Is there [a matinée] today?
Есть ли сегодня [дневной спектакль]?
YEHST^y-l^yee s^yih-VOHD-n^yuh [dn^yihv-NOY sp^yihk-TAH-kuhl^y]?

1124. Has [the show] begun?
[Спектакль] уже начался?
[sp^yihk-TAH-kuhl^y] oo-ZHEH nuh-chihl-SAH?

1125. What is playing now?
Что идёт сейчас? *shtoh ee-D^yOHT s^yih-CHAHS?*

1126. Have you any seats for tonight?
Есть у вас места на сегодняшний вечер?
yehst^y oo-VAHS m^yih-STAH nuh-s^yih-VOHD-n^yihsh-n^yee V^yEH-chihr?

1127. How much is [an orchestra seat]?
Сколько стоит [место в партере]?
SKOHL^y-kuh STOH-yiht [M^yEH-stuh fpahr-TEH-r^yih]?

1128. —a balcony seat.
—место на балконе.
—M^yEH-stuh nuh-bahl-KOH-n^yih.

1129. —a box seat.
—место в ложе. *—M^yEH-stuh VLOH-zhï.*

1130. —a seat in the mezzanine (newer theaters/older theaters).
—место в амфитеатре/в бельэтаже.
—M^yEH-stuh vahm-f^yee-t^yih-AH-tr^yih/ vbeh-leh-TAH-zhï.

1131. Not too far from the stage.
Не слишком далеко от сцены.
n^yih-SL^yEESH-kuhm duh-l^yih-KOH ahts-TSEH-nï.

1132. Here is my ticket.
Вот мой билет. *voht moy b^yee-L^yEHT.*

1133. Can I see and hear well from there?
Хорошо видно и слышно оттуда?
*khuh-rah-SHOH V^yEED-nuh ee SLÏSH-nuh
aht-TOO-duh?*

1134. Follow [the usher].
Следуйте за [билетёром].
SL^yEH-doo‿ee-t^yih zuh-[b^yee-l^yih-T^yOH-ruhm].

1135. Is smoking permitted here?
Здесь можно курить?
zd^yehs^y MOHZH-nuh koo-R^yEET^y?

1136. How long is the intermission?
Как долго будет антракт?
kahk DOHL-guh BOO-d^yiht ahn-TRAHKT?

1137. When does the program [begin] [end]?
Когда [начнётся] [кончится] спектакль?
*kahg-DAH [nahch-N^yOHT-tsuh] [KOHN-chiht-tsuh]
sp^yihk-TAH-kuhl^y?*

1138. Everyone enjoyed the show.
Спектакль всем понравился.
sp^yihk-TAH-kuhl^y fs^yehm pah-NRAH-v^yeel-suh.

1139. The ballet. Балет. *bah-L^yEHT.*

1140. The box office. Касса. *KAHS-suh.*

1141. The circus. Цирк. *tsïrk.*

1142. The concert. Концерт. *kahn-TSEHRT.*

1143. The folk dances.
Народные танцы. *nah-ROHD-nï-yih TAHN-tsï.*

1144. The [beginning] [end] of the line.
[Начало] [Конец] очереди.
[nah-CHAH-luh] [kah-N^yEHTS] OH-chih-r^yih-d^yee.

1145. The movies. Кино́. *k^{y}ee-NOH.*

1146. The musical comedy (OR: **Operetta**).
Музыка́льная коме́дия (OR: Опере́тта).
moo-zï-KAHL^y-nuh-yuh kah-M^{y}EH-d^{y}ee-yuh
(OR: *ah-p^{y}ih-R^{y}EH-tuh*).

1147. The nightclub.
Ночно́й клуб. *nahch-NOY kloop.*

1148. The orchestra. Орке́стр. *ahr-K^{y}EHS-tuhr.*

1149. The opera. О́пера. *OH-p^{y}ih-ruh.*

1150. The opera glasses. Бино́кль. *b^{y}ee-NOH-kuhl^y.*

1151. The opera house.
О́перный теа́тр. *OH-p^{y}ihr-nï␣ee t^{y}ih-AH-tuhr.*

1152. The performance.
Представле́ние. *pr^{y}iht-stahv-L^{y}EH-n^{y}ee-yuh.*

1153. The program.
Програ́мма. *prah-GRAHM-muh.*

1154. The puppet show.
Ку́кольный спекта́кль.
KOO-kuhl^y-nï␣ee sp^{y}ihk-TAH-kuhl^y.

1155. The reserved seat.
Заброни́рованное ме́сто.
zuh-brah-N^{y}EE-ruh-vuhn-nuh-yuh M^{y}EH-stuh.

1156. The sports event.
Спорти́вное соревнова́ние.
spahr-T^{y}EEV-nuh-yuh suh-r^{y}ihv-nah-VAH-n^{y}ee-yuh.

1157. Standing room (LIT.: **An admission ticket without seat**).
Входно́й биле́т без ме́ста.
fkhad-NOY b^{y}ee-L^{y}EHT b^{y}ihz-M^{y}EH-stuh.

1158. The theater. Теа́тр. *t^{y}ih-AH-tuhr.*

1159. The ticket window.

(Билéтная) кácса.

(*b*ʸ*ee-L*ʸ*EHT-nuh-yuh*) *KAHS-suh.*

1160. The variety show.

Теáтр-варьетé. *t*ʸ*ih-AH-tuhr–vahr*ʸ*-yeh-TEH.*

NIGHTCLUB AND DANCING

1161. How much is [the admission charge]?

Скóлько стóит [входнóй билéт]?

*SKOHL*ʸ*-kuh STOH-yiht* [*fkhahd-NOY b*ʸ*ee-L*ʸ*EHT*]?

1162. What is the minimum charge?

Какáя бýдет минимáльная ценá билéта?

*kah-KAH-yuh BOO-d*ʸ*iht m*ʸ*ee-n*ʸ*ee-MAHL*ʸ*-nuh-yuh*
 *ts*ï*-NAH b*ʸ*ee-L*ʸ*EH-tuh?*

1163. Is there a floor show?

Бýдет представлéние (OR: концéрт)?

*BOO-d*ʸ*iht pr*ʸ*iht-stahv-L*ʸ*EH-n*ʸ*ee-yuh* (OR: *kahn-
TSEHRT*)?

1164. Where can we go to dance?

Гдé мóжно потанцевáть?

*gd*ʸ*eh MOHZH-nuh puh-tuhn-tsï-VAHT*ʸ?

1165. May I have this dance?

Разрешúте (пригласúть вáс на э́тот тáнец).

*ruhz-r*ʸ*ih-SHĬ-t*ʸ*ih* (*pr*ʸ*ee-glah-S*ʸ*EET*ʸ *vahs nah-EH-tuht
TAH-n*ʸ*ihts*).

1166. You dance very well.

Вы óчень хорошó тáнцуете.

*vï OH-chihn*ʸ *khuh-rah-SHOH tahn-TSOO-yih-t*ʸ*ih.*

1167. Will you play [a fox-trot]?
Пожа́луйста, сыгра́йте [фокстро́т].
pah-ZHAH-lï-stuh, sï-GRAH͜EE-t ʸih [fahks-TROHT].

1168. —a rumba. —ру́мбу. *—ROOM-boo.*

1169. —a samba. —са́мбу. *—SAHM-boo.*

1170. —a tango. —танго́. *—tahn-GOH.*

1171. —a waltz. —ва́льс. *—vahl ʸs.*

1172. —a folk dance.
—наро́дный та́нец. *—nah-ROHD-nï͜ee TAH-n ʸihts.*

1173. —rock music.
—рок-н-ро́лл. *—roh-kuhn-ROHL.*

SPORTS AND GAMES

1174. We want to play [soccer].
Мы хоти́м игра́ть [в футбо́л].
mï khah-T ʸEEM ee-GRAHT ʸ [ffood-BOHL].

1175. —basketball.
—в баскетбо́л. *—vbuhs-k ʸihd-BOHL.*

1176. —cards. —в ка́рты. *—FKAHR-tï.*

1177. —ping-pong.
—в пинг-по́нг. *—fp ʸeenk-POHNK.*

1178. —tennis. —в те́ннис. *—FTEH-n ʸees.*

1179. —volleyball.
—в волейбо́л. *—vvuh-l ʸih͜ee-BOHL.*

1180. Do you play [chess]?
Вы игра́ете [в ша́хматы]?
vï ee-GRAH-yih-t ʸih [FSHAHKH-muh-tï]?

1181. —checkers. —в ша́шки. *—FSHAHSH-k ʸee.*

1182. —bridge. —в бри́дж. *—vbr ʸeech.*

1183. Let's go swimming.
Пойдёмте купа́ться.
pah ̮ ee-D^yOHM-t^yih koo-PAHT-tsuh.

1184. Let's go [to the swimming pool].
Пойдёмте [в пла́вательный бассе́йн].
pah ̮ ee-D^yOHM-t^yih [FPLAH-vuh-t^yihl^y-nï ̮ ee bah-S^yEH ̮ EEN].

1185. —to the beach.
—на пляж. —*nah-PL^yAHSH.*

1186. —to the horse races.
—на ска́чки. —*nah-SKAHCH-k^yee.*

1187. —to the soccer game.
—на футбо́льный ма́тч.
—*nuh-food-BOHL^y-nï ̮ ee mahch.*

1188. I need fishing tackle.
Мне́ нужны́ рыболо́вные сна́сти.
mn^yeh noozh-NÏ rï-bah-LOHV-nï-yih SNAH-st^yee.

1189. I need a tennis racket.
Мне́ нужна́ те́ннисная раке́тка.
mn^yeh noozh-NAH TEH-n^yees-nuh-yuh rah-K^yEHT-kuh.

1190. Can we go [fishing]? (LIT.: **Do you have anywhere [to go fishing]?**)
У ва́с есть где́ [лови́ть ры́бу]?
oo-VAHS yehst^y gd^yeh [lah-V^yEET^y RÏ-boo]?

1191. —boating.
—ката́ться на ло́дке.
—*kah-TAHT-tsuh nah-LOHT-k^yih.*

1192. —horseback riding.
—е́здить верхо́м. —*YEHZ-d^yeet^y v^yihr-KHOHM.*

1193. —roller skating.
—ката́ться на ро́ликах.
—*kah-TAHT-tsuh nah-ROH-l^yee-kuhkh.*

1194. —ice skating.
—кататься на коньках.
—*kah-TAHT-tsuh nuh-kahn^y-KAHKH.*

1195. —sledding.
—кататься на санках.
—*kah-TAHT-tsuh nah-SAHN-kuhkh.*

1196. —skiing.
—кататься на лыжах.
—*kah-TAHT-tsuh nah-LĬ-zhuhkh.*

HIKING AND CAMPING

1197. How long a walk is it to the youth hostel?
Как долго идти пешком в молодёжное общежитие?
kahk DOHL-guh eet-T^yEE p^yihsh-KOHM vmuh-lah-
D^yOHZH-nuh-yuh ahp-shhih-ZHĬ-t^yee-yuh?

1198. Are sanitary facilities available?
Есть ли санитарные удобства?
YEHST^y-l^yee suh-n^yee-TAHR-nï-yih oo-DOHP-stvuh?

1199. Campsite. Кемпинг. *KEHM-p^yeenk.*

1200. Camping equipment.
Оборудование кемпинга.
ah-bah-ROO-duh-vuh-n^yee-yuh KEHM-p^yeen-guh.

1201. Camping permit.
Пропуск в кемпинг.
PROH-poosk FKEHM-p^yeenk.

1202. Cooking utensils.
Кухонная посуда. *KOO-khuhn-nuh-yuh pah-SOO-duh.*

1203. Firewood. Дрова. *drah-VAH.*

1204. Footpath. Тропинка. *trah-P^yEEN-kuh.*

1205. Hike. Прогу́лка. *prah-GOOL-kuh.*

1206. Picnic. Пикни́к. *p^yeek-N^yEEK.*

1207. Rubbish. Му́сор. *MOO-suhr.*

1208. Rubbish receptacle.
Му́сорный я́щик. *MOO-suhr-nï ̮ee YAH-shheek.*

1209. Shortcut.
Пу́ть напрями́к. *poot^y nuh-pr^yih-M^yEEK.*

1210. Tent. Пала́тка. *pah-LAHT-kuh.*

1211. Thermos Те́рмос. *TEHR-muhs.*

1212. Drinking water.
Питьева́я вода́. *p^yeet^y-yih-VAH-yuh vah-DAH.*

1213. Forest. Ле́с. *l^yehs.*

1214. Lake. О́зеро. *OH-z^yih-ruh.*

1215. Mountain. Гора́. *gah-RAH.*

1216. River. Река́. *r^yih-KAH.*

1217. Stream. Ре́чка. *R^yEHCH-kuh.*

BANK AND MONEY

1218. Where can I change foreign money?
Где́ мо́жно обменя́ть валю́ту?
gd^yeh MOHZH-nuh ahb-m^yih-N^yAHT^y vah-L^yOO-too?

1219. What is the exchange rate on the dollar?
Како́й сейча́с обме́нный ку́рс до́ллара?
kah-KOY s^yih-CHAHS ahb-M^yEHN-nï ̮ee koors DOHL-luh-ruh?

1220. Will you cash [a personal check]?
Вы дади́те мне нали́чные по [ли́чному че́ку]?
vï dah-D^yEE-t^yih mn^yeh nah-L^yEECH-nï-yih pah [L^yEECH-nuh-moo CHEH-koo]?

1221. —a traveler's check.

—доро́жному че́ку.

—*dah-ROHZH-nuh-moo CHEH-koo.*

1222. I have [a bank draft].

У меня́ [ба́нковский че́к на моё и́мя].

*oo-m^{y}ih-N^{y}AH [BAHN-kuhf-sk^{y}ee chehk nuh-mah-YOH
EE-m^{y}uh].*

1223. —a letter of credit.

—аккредити́в.   —*ah-kr^{y}ih-d^{y}ee-T^{y}EEF.*

1224. I would like to exchange [twenty] dollars.

Я хоте́л (F.: хоте́ла) бы обменя́ть [два́дцать]
до́лларов.

*yah khah-T^{y}EHL (F.: khah-T^{y}EH-luh)-bï ahb-m^{y}ih-
N^{y}AHT^y [DVAHT-tsuht^y] DOHL-luh-ruhf.*

1225. Please give me [large bills].

Да́йте мне, пожа́луйста, [кру́пными купю́рами].

*DAH _ EE-t^{y}ih mn^{y}eh, pah-ZHAH-lï-stuh,
[KROOP-nï-m^{y}ee koo-P^{y}OO-ruh-m^{y}ee].*

1226. —small bills.

—ме́лкими купю́рами.

—*M^{y}EHL-k^{y}ee-m^{y}ee koo-P^{y}OO-ruh-m^{y}ee.*

1227. —small change.

—ме́лкими моне́тами.

—*M^{y}EHL-k^{y}ee-m^{y}ee mah-N^{y}EH-tuh-m^{y}ee.*

SHOPPING

1228. Show me [the hat] in the window.

Покажи́те мне [шля́пу] в витри́не.

*puh-kah-ZHÏ-t^{y}ih mn^{y}eh [SHL^{y}AH-poo] vv^{y}ee-
TR^{y}EE-n^{y}ih.*

1229. Can you [help me]?
Вы можете [мне помочь]?
vï MOH-zhuh-t^yih [mn^yeh pah-MOHCH]?

1230. I am just looking around.
Я только присматриваю.
yah TOHL^y-kuh pr^yee-SMAH-tr^yee-vuh-yoo.

1231. I shall come back later.
Я вернусь позже. *yah v^yihr-NOOS^y POH-zhhih.*

1232. I've been waiting [a long time].
Я [давно] жду. *yah [dahv-NOH] zhdoo.*

1233. —a short time.
—недолго. *—n^yih-DOHL-guh.*

1234. What brand do you have?
Какая у вас марка?
kah-KAH-yuh oo-VAHS MAHR-kuh?

1235. How much is it [per gram]?
Сколько стоит [грамма]?
SKOHL^y-kuh STOH-yiht [GRAHM-muh]?

1236. —per piece. —штука. *—SHTOO-kuh.*

1237. —per meter. —метр. *—M^yEH-tuhr.*

1238. —per pound. —фунт. *—foont.*

1239. —per kilo. —кило. *—k^yee-LOH.*

1240. —per package.
—пакет (OR: пачка).
—pah-K^yEHT (OR: PAHCH-kuh).

1241. —per bunch. —пучок. *—poo-CHOHK.*

1242. —all together.
—всё вместе. *—fs^yoh VM^yEH-st^yih.*

1243. It is [too expensive].
Это [слишком дорого].
EH-tuh [SL^yEESH-kuhm DOH-ruh-guh].

1244. —cheap. —дёшево. —*D^yOH-shuh-vuh.*

1245. —reasonable. —хорошо́. —*khuh-rah-SHOH.*

1246. Is that your lowest price?
Это ва́ша са́мая ни́зкая цена́?
EH-tuh VAH-shuh SAH-muh-yuh N^yEES-kuh-yuh tsï-NAH?

1247. Do you give a discount?
Вы даёте ски́дку? *vï dah-YOH-t^yih SK^yEET-koo?*

1248. I [do not] like that.
Это мне [не] нра́вится.
EH-tuh mn^yeh [n^yih]-NRAH-v^yiht-tsuh.

1249. Have you something [better]?
Есть ли у вас что́-нибудь [полу́чше]?
YEHST^y-l^yee oo-VAHS SHTOH-n^yee-boot^y [pah-LOOCH-shï]?

1250. —cheaper.
—подеше́вле. —*puh-d^yih-SHEHV-l^yih.*

1251. —more fashionable.
—помо́днее. —*pah-MOHD-n^yih-yih.*

1252. —softer. —помя́гче. —*pah-M^yAHKH-chih.*

1253. —stronger. —покре́пче. —*pah-KR^yEHP-chih.*

1254. —heavier.
—потяжеле́е. —*puh-t^yih-zhï-L^yEH-yih.*

1255. —lighter (in weight).
—поле́гче. —*pah-L^yEHKH-chih.*

1256. —tighter. —поу́же. —*pah-OO-zhï.*

1257. —looser.
—посвобо́днее. —*puh-svah-BOHD-n^yih-yih.*

1258. —lighter (in color).
—посветле́е. —*puh-sv^yiht-L^yEH-yih.*

1259. —darker.

—потемнее.   —*puh-t^yihm-N^yEH-yih.*

1260. Do you have this in [my size]?

У вас есть это [моего размера]?

*oo-VAHS yehst^y EH-tuh [muh-yih-VOH
rahz-M^yEH-ruh]?*

1261. —a larger size.

—большего размера.

—*BOHL^y-shuh-vuh rahz-M^yEH-ruh.*

1262. —a smaller size.

—меньшего размера.

—*M^yEHN^y-shuh-vuh rahz-M^yEH-ruh.*

1263. Can I order it in [another color]?

Можно это заказать [другого цвета]?

*MOHZH-nuh EH-tuh zuh-kah-ZAHT^y [droo-GOH-vuh
TSV^yEH-tuh]?*

1264. —a different style.

—другого фасона.   —*droo-GOH-vuh fah-SOH-nuh.*

1265. Where is the fitting room?

Где примерочная?

gd^yeh pr^yee-M^yEH-ruhch-nuh-yuh?

1266. May I try it on?

Можно это примерить?

MOHZH-nuh EH-tuh pr^yee-M^yEH-r^yeet^y?

1267. It does not fit.

Это не подходит по размеру.

EH-tuh n^yih-paht-KHOH-d^yiht puh-rahz-M^yEH-roo.

1268. Too short.

Слишком коротко.   *SL^yEESH-kuhm KOH-ruht-kuh.*

1269. Too long.

Слишком длинно.   *SL^yEESH-kuhm DL^yEEN-nuh.*

1270. Too big.
Слишком велико.   *SL^yEESH-kuhm v^yih-l^yee-KOH.*

1271. Too small.
Слишком мало́.   *SL^yEESH-kuhm mah-LOH.*

1272. Please take my measurements.
Пожа́луйста, сними́те с меня́ ме́рку.
*pah-ZHAH-lï-stuh, sn^yee-M^yEE-t^yih sm^yih-N^yAH
M^yEHR-koo.*

1273. The length. Длина́. *dl^yee-NAH.*

1274. The width. Ширина́. *shï-r^yee-NAH.*

1275. Will it shrink? (LIT.: **Won't it shrink?**)
Не ся́дет ли э́то?
n^yih-S^yAH-d^yiht-l^yee EH-tuh?

1276. Will it break? (LIT.: **Won't it break?**)
Не разобьётся ли э́то?
n^yih-ruh-zah-B^yYOHT-tsuh-l^yee EH-tuh?

1277. Is this colorfast? (LIT.: **Won't it discolor?**)
Не полиня́ет ли э́то?
n^yih-puh-l^yee-N^yAH-yiht-l^yee EH-tuh?

1278. Is it [new]?
Э́то [но́вое]? *EH-tuh [NOH-vuh-yuh]?*

1279. —handmade.
—ручно́й рабо́ты. *—rooch-NOY rah-BOH-tï.*

1280. —an antique.
—антиква́рная вещь.
—ahn-t^yee-KVAHR-nuh-yuh v^yehshh.

1281. —a replica. —ко́пия. *—KOH-p^yee-yuh.*

1282. —an imitation.
—имита́ция. *—ee-m^yee-TAH-tsï-yuh.*

1283. —secondhand.
—подержанное. —*pah-D^yEHR-zhuhn-nuh-yuh.*

1284. This is [not] my size.
Это [не] моего размера.
EH-tuh [n^yih]-muh-yih-VOH rahz-M^yEH-ruh.

1285. Please have this ready soon.
Пожалуйста, приготовьте это поскорее.
*pah-ZHAH-li-stuh, pr^yee-gah-TOHF^y-t^yih EH-tuh
puh-skah-R^yEH-yih.*

1286. How long will it take to make the alterations?
Сколько времени займёт переделка?
*SKOHL^y-kuh VR^yEH-m^yih-n^yee zah̲ ee-M^yOHT
p^yih-r^yih-D^yEHL-kuh?*

1287. Does the price include alterations?
Входит ли в цену переделка?
FKHOH-d^yiht-l^yee FTSEH-noo p^yih-r^yih-D^yEHL-kuh?

1288. I cannot decide.
Я не могу решить. *yah n^yih-mah-GOO r^yih-SHÏT^y.*

1289. I'll wait until it is ready.
Я подожду, пока это (не) будет готово.
*yah puh-dahzh-DOO, pah-KAH EH-tuh (n^yih)-BOO-d^yiht
gah-TOH-vuh.*

1290. Wrap this.
Заверните это. *zuh-v^yihr-N^yEE-t^yih EH-tuh.*

1291. Where do I pay? Где касса? *gd^yeh KAHS-suh?*

1292. Do I pay [the salesman]?
Мне платить [продавцу]?
mn^yeh plah-T^yEET^y [pruh-dahf-TSOO]?

1293. —the salesgirl.
—продавщице. —*pruh-dahf-SHHEE-tsï.*

1294. —the cashier.
—касси́ру (F.: касси́рше).
—*kahs-S^yEE-roo* (F.: *kahs-S^yEER-shï*).

1295. Will you honor this credit card?
Принима́ете ли вы э́ту креди́тную ка́рточку?
pr^yee-n^yee-MAH-yih-t^yih-l^yee vï EH-too kr^yih-D^yEET-noo-yoo KAHR-tuhch-koo?

1296. May I pay with [a personal check]?
Мо́жно плати́ть [ли́чным че́ком]?
MOHZH-nuh plah-T^yEET^y [L^yEECH-nïm CHEH-kuhm]?

1297. —a traveler's check.
—доро́жным че́ком.
—dah-ROHZH-nïm CHEH-kuhm.

1298. Is this identification acceptable?
Годи́тся ли э́то удостовере́ние ли́чности?
gah-D^yEET-tsuh-l^yee EH-tuh oo-duh-stuh-v^yih-R^yEH-n^yee-yuh L^yEECH-nuh-st^yee?

1299. Is this reference sufficient?
Доста́точна ли э́та рекоменда́ция?
dah-STAH-tuhch-nuh-l^yee EH-tuh r^yih-kuh-m^yihn-DAH-tsï-yuh?

1300. Can you send it to my hotel?
Мо́жно э́то посла́ть в мою́ гости́ницу?
MOHZH-nuh EH-tuh pah-SLAHT^y vmah-YOO gah-ST^yEE-n^yee-tsoo?

1301. Can you ship it [to New York City]?
Мо́жно э́то посла́ть [в Нью-Йо́рк]?
MOHZH-nuh EH-tuh pah-SLAHT^y [vn^yyoo-YOHRK]?

1302. Pack this carefully for export.

Упакуйте это как следует для отправки за границу.

*oo-pah-KOO___EE-t*ʸ*ih EH-tuh kahk SL*ʸ*EH-doo-yiht*
  *dl*ʸ*ah-aht-PRAHF-k*ʸ*ee zuh-grah-N*ʸ*EE-tsoo.*

1303. Give me [a bill].

Дайте мне [счёт]. *DAH___EE-t*ʸ*ih mn*ʸ*eh [shhoht].*

1304. —a receipt.

—квитанцию. *—kv*ʸ*ee-TAHN-ts*ĭ*-yoo.*

1305. —a credit memo.

—копию счёта по кредиту.

*—KOH-p*ʸ*ee-yoo SHHOH-tuh puh-kr*ʸ*ih-D*ʸ*EE-too.*

1306. I shall pay upon delivery.

Я оплачу при доставке.

*yah ah-PLAH-choo pr*ʸ*ee-dah-STAHF-k*ʸ*ih.*

1307. Is there an additional charge for delivery?

Будет ли дополнительная плата за доставку?

*BOO-d*ʸ*iht-l*ʸ*ee duh-pahl-N*ʸ*EE-t*ʸ*ihl*ʸ*-nuh-yuh*
  PLAH-tuh zuh-dah-STAHF-koo?

1308. I wish to return this.

Я хочу вернуть это.

*yah khah-CHOO v*ʸ*ihr-NOOT*ʸ *EH-tuh.*

1309. Refund my money.

Возвратите мне деньги.

*vuhz-vrah-T*ʸ*EE-t*ʸ*ih mn*ʸ*eh D*ʸ*EHN*ʸ*-g*ʸ*ee.*

1310. Please exchange this.

Пожалуйста, обменяйте это.

*pah-ZHAH-lĭ-stuh, ahb-m*ʸ*ih-N*ʸ*AH___EE-t*ʸ*ih EH-tuh.*

CLOTHING AND ACCESSORIES

1311. A bathing cap.
Купа́льная ша́почка.
koo-PAHL^y-nuh-yuh SHAH-puhch-kuh.

1312. A bathing suit.
Купа́льный костю́м.
koo-PAHL^y-nï ̮ee kah-ST^yOOM.

1313. A blouse. Блу́зка. *BLOOS-kuh.*

1314. An elastic belt.
Эласти́чный по́яс. *eh-lah-ST^yEECH-nï ̮ee POH-yihs.*

1315. Boots. Сапоги́. *suh-pah-G^yEE.*

1316. Bracelet. Брасле́т. *brahs-L^yEHT.*

1317. Brassiere.
Бюстга́льтер. *b^yooz-GAHL^y-tehr.*

1318. A button. Пу́говица. *POO-guh-v^yee-tsuh.*

1319. A cane. Тро́сть. *trohst^y.*

1320. A cap. Ша́пка. *SHAHP-kuh.*

1321. A coat. Пальто́. *pahl^y-TOH.*

1322. A collar. Воротни́к. *vuh-raht-N^yEEK.*

1323. A compact. Пу́дреница. *POO-dr^yih-n^yee-tsuh.*

1324. Cufflinks. За́понки. *ZAH-puhn-k^yee.*

1325. A dress. Пла́тье. *PLAHT^y-yuh.*

1326. Earrings. Се́рьги. *S^yEHR^y-g^yee.*

1327. A pair of gloves.
Па́ра перча́ток. *PAH-ruh p^yihr-CHAH-tuhk.*

1328. A handbag. Су́мка. *SOOM-kuh.*

1329. Handkerchiefs.
Носовы́е платки́. *nuh-sah-VЇ-yih plaht-K^yEE.*

1330. A jacket (men's dress jacket/women's dress jacket/ windbreaker).
Пиджа́к/Жаке́т/Ку́ртка.
p^yee-JAHK/zhah-K^yEHT/KOORT-kuh.

1331. A dinner jacket.
Смо́кинг. *SMOH-k^yeenk.*

1332. A necktie. Га́лстук. *GAHL-stook.*

1333. Lingerie.
Да́мское бельё. *DAHM-skuh-yuh b^yihl^y-YOH.*

1334. A money clip.
Де́нежная скре́пка.
D^yEH-n^yihzh-nuh-yuh SKR^yEHP-kuh.

1335. A nightgown.
Ночна́я соро́чка. *nahch-NAH-yuh sah-ROHCH-kuh.*

1336. Pajamas. Пижа́ма. *p^yee-ZHAH-muh.*

1337. Panties. Тру́сики. *TROO-s^yee-k^yee.*

1338. A pin (decorative).
Значо́к. *znah-CHOHK.*

1339. Brooch.
Бро́шь (OR: Бро́шка).   *brohsh* (OR: *BROHSH-kuh*).

1340. A pin (common). Шпи́лька. *SHP^yEEL^y-kuh.*

1341. A safety pin.
Англи́йская була́вка.
ahn-GL^yEE-skuh-yuh boo-LAHF-kuh.

1342. A raincoat. Пла́щ. *plahshh.*

1343. Ribbon. Ле́нта. *L^yEHN-tuh.*

1344. A ring.
Кольцо́ (OR: Пе́рстень).
kahl^y-TSOH (OR: *P^yEHR-st^yihn^y*).

1345. Rubbers. Гало́ши. *gah-LOH-shï.*

1346. Sandals. Сандáлии. *sahn-DAHL-lʸee-yee.*

1347. A lady's scarf.
Жéнский шáрф. *ZHEHN-skʸee shahrf.*

1348. A man's scarf.
Мужскóй шáрф. *moosh-SKOY shahrf.*

1349. A shawl. Шáль. *shahlʸ.*

1350. A shirt. Рубáшка. *roo-BAHSH-kuh.*

1351. Shoelaces. Шнýрки. *SHNOOR-kʸee.*

1352. Shoes. Тýфли. *TOOF-lʸee.*

1353. Slippers. Тáпочки. *TAH-puhch-kʸee.*

1354. Socks. Носки́. *nah-SKʸEE.*

1355. Walking shorts [for men].
Шóрты [для мужчи́н].
SHOHR-tï [dlʸuh-moo-SHHEEN].

1356. A skirt. Ю́бка. *YOOP-kuh.*

1357. A slip. Комбинáция (OR: Ни́жняя ю́бка).
kuhm-bʸee-NAH-tsï-yuh (OR: *Nʸ EEZH-nʸuh-yuh YOOP-kuh.*).

1358. Stockings. Чулки́. *chool-Kʸ EE.*

1359. A strap. Ремéнь. *rʸih-MʸEHNʸ.*

1360. A man's suit.
Мужскóй костю́м. *moosh-SKOY kah-STʸOOM.*

1361. A sweater (crew neck/man's V-neck/cardigan).
Сви́тер/Пулóвер/Кóфта.
SVʸ EE-tʸihr/poo-LOH-vʸihr/KOHF-tuh.

1362. A pair of trousers. Брю́ки. *BRʸOO-kʸee.*

1363. Man's underwear.
Мужскóе ни́жнее бельё.
moosh-SKOH-yuh Nʸ EEZH-nʸuh-yuh bʸihlʸ-YOH.

1364. An umbrella. Зóнтик. *ZOHN-t^{y}eek.*

1365. An undershirt (sleeveless/with sleeves).
Мáйка/Ни́жняя рубáшка.
MAH‿EE-kuh/N^{y}EEZH-n^{y}uh-yuh roo-BAHSH-kuh.

1366. Undershorts. Трусы́. *troo-SЇ.*

1367. A watchband. Ремешóк. *r^{y}ih-m^{y}ih-SHOHK.*

COLORS

1368. Black. Чёрный. *CHOHR-nï‿ee.*

1369. Light blue. Голубóй. *guh-loo-BOY.*

1370. Dark blue. Си́ний. *S^{y}EE-n^{y}ee.*

1371. Brown. Кори́чневый. *kah-R^{y}EECH-n^{y}ih-vï‿ee.*

1372. Gray. Сéрый. *S^{y}EH-rï‿ee.*

1373. Green. Зелёный. *z^{y}ih-L^{y}OH-nï‿ee.*

1374. Olive green (OR: **Khaki**).
Оли́вковый (OR: Хáки).
ah-L^{y}EEF-kuh-vï‿ee (OR: *KHAH-k^{y}ee*).

1375. Orange. Орáнжевый. *ah-RAHN-zhuh-vï‿ee.*

1376. Pink. Рóзовый. *ROH-zuh-vï‿ee.*

1377. Purple. Пурпýрный. *poor-POOR-nï‿ee.*

1378. Violet. Фиолéтовый. *f^{y}ee-ah-L^{y}EH-tuh-vï‿ee.*

1379. Red. Крáсный. *KRAHS-nï‿ee.*

1380. Tan.
Желтевàто-кори́чневый.
zhuhl-t^{y}ih-VAH-tuh–kah-R^{y}EECH-n^{y}ih-vï‿ee.

1381. White. Бéлый. *B^{y}EH-lï‿ee.*

1382. Yellow. Жёлтый. *ZHOHL-tï‿ee.*

MATERIALS

1383. Metal. Металл. *mᵧih-TAHL.*

1384. Aluminum.
Алюминий. *ah-lᵧoo-Mᵧ EE-nᵧee.*

1385. Brass. Латунь. *lah-TOONᵧ.*

1386. Copper. Медь. *mᵧehtᵧ.*

1387. Gold. Золото. *ZOH-luh-tuh.*

1388. Iron. Железо. *zhĭ-Lᵧ EH-zuh.*

1389. Silver. Серебро. *sᵧih-rᵧih-BROH.*

1390. Steel. Сталь. *stahlᵧ.*

1391. Textiles. Текстиль. *tᵧihk-STᵧ EELᵧ.*

1392. Cotton.
Хлопчатобумажная ткань.
khlahp-CHAH-tuh-boo-MAHZH-nuh-yuh tkahnᵧ.

1393. Dacron. Дакрон. *dah-KROHN.*

1394. Nylon. Нейлон. *nᵧih‿ee-LOHN.*

1395. Orlon. Орлон. *ahr-LOHN.*

1396. Silk. Шёлк. *shohlk.*

1397. Synthetic.
Синтетика. *sᵧeen-Tᵧ EH-tᵧee-kuh.*

1398. Wool. Шёрсть. *shehrstᵧ.*

1399. Ceramics. Керамика. *kᵧih-RAH-mᵧee-kuh.*

1400. China. Фарфор. *fahr-FOHR.*

1401. Crystal. Хрусталь. *khroo-STAHLᵧ.*

1402. Fur. Мех. *mᵧehkh.*

1403. Glass. Стекло. *stᵧih-KLOH.*

1404. Leather. Кожа. *KOH-zhuh.*

1405. Plastic. Пластма́сса. *plahst-MAHS-suh.*

1406. Stone. Ка́мень. *KAH-m^{y}ihn^y.*

1407. Wood. Де́рево. *D^{y}EH-r^{y}ih-vuh.*

BOOKSHOP, STATIONER, NEWSDEALER

1408. Do you have [any books] in English?
У ва́с е́сть [кни́ги] на англи́йском языке́?
oo-VAHS yehst^y [KN^{y}EE-g^{y}ee] nah-ahn-GL^{y}EE-skuhm yih-zï-K^{y}EH?

1409. I am just browsing.
Я то́лько присма́триваю.
yah TOHL^y-kuh pr^{y}ee-SMAH-tr^{y}ee-vuh-yoo.

1410. Playing cards.
Игра́льные ка́рты. *ee-GRAHL^y-nï-yih KAHR-tï.*

1411. A dictionary. Слова́рь. *slah-VAHR^y.*

1412. A package of 10 envelopes.
Деся́тка конве́ртов.
d^{y}ih-S^{y}AHT-kuh kahn-V^{y}EHR-tuhf.

1413. An eraser. Рези́нка. *r^{y}ih-Z^{y}EEN-kuh.*

1414. Fiction.
Худо́жественная литерату́ра.
khoo-DOH-zhuh-stv^{y}ihn-nuh-yuh l^{y}ee-t^{y}ih-rah-TOO-ruh.

1415. Folders. Па́пки. *PAHP-k^{y}ee.*

1416. A guidebook.
Путеводи́тель. *poo-t^{y}ih-vah-D^{y}EE-t^{y}ihl^y.*

1417. Ink. Черни́ла. *chihr-N^{y}EE-luh.*

1418. A map. Ка́рта. *KAHR-tuh.*

1419. Some magazines. Журна́лы. *zhoor-NAH-lï.*

1420. A newspaper. Газе́та. *gah-Z^yEH-tuh.*

1421. Nonfiction.
Документа́льная литерату́ра.
duh-koo-m^yihn-TAHL^y-nuh-yuh l^yee-t^yih-rah-TOO-ruh.

1422. A notebook. Тетра́дь. *t^yih-TRAHT^y.*

1423. Airmail stationery.
А̀виапочто́вый набо́р.
AH-v^yee-uh-pahch-TOH-vï__ee nah-BOHR.

1424. Notepaper (LIT.: **Lined paper**).
Лино́ванная бума́га.
l^yee-NOH-vuhn-nuh-yuh boo-MAH-guh.

1425. Notepad. Блокно́т. *blahk-NOHT.*

1426. Carbon paper. Копи́рка. *kah-P^yEER-kuh.*

1427. Writing paper.
Почто́вая бума́га. *pahch-TOH-vuh-yuh boo-MAH-guh.*

1428. A fountain pen.
Авторучка. *ahf-tah-ROOCH-kuh.*

1429. A ballpoint pen.
Ша́риковая ру́чка.
SHAH-r^yee-kuh-vuh-yuh ROOCH-kuh.

1430. A pencil. Каранда́ш. *kuh-rahn-DAHSH.*

1431. Tape. Ле́нта. *L^yEHN-tuh.*

1432. Scotch tape.
Скле́ивающая ле́нта (OR: Ско́тч).
SKL^yEH-yee-vuh-yoo-shhuh-yuh L^yEHN-tuh
   (OR: *skohch*).

1433. String. Верёвка. *v^yih-R^yOHF-kuh.*

1434. A typewriter.

Пишущая машинка.

P^yEE-shoo-shhuh-yuh mah-SHĬN-kuh.

1435. Typewriter ribbon.

Лента для пишущей машинки.

L^yEHN-tuh dl^yah-P^yEE-shoo-shhih‿ee mah-SHĬN-k^yee.

1436. Wrapping paper.

Обёрточная бумага.

ah-B^yOHR-tuhch-nuh-yuh boo-MAH-guh.

PHARMACY

1437. Is there [a pharmacy] here where they understand English?

Есть ли здесь [аптека], где понимают по-английски?

YEHST^y-l^yee zd^yehs^y [ahp-T^yEH-kuh], gd^yeh puh-n^yee-MAH-yoot pah-ahn-GL^yEE-sk^yee?

1438. May I speak to [a clerk]?

Можно говорить с [продавцом (F.: продавщицей)]?

MOHZH-nuh guh-vah-R^yEET^y s[pruh-dahf-TSOHM (F.: pruh-dahf-SHHEE-tsuh‿ee)]?

1439. Can you fill this prescription [immediately]?

Сможете ли вы приготовить лекарство по этому рецепту [сейчас]?

SMOH-zhuh-t^yih-l^yee vï pr^yee-gah-TOH-v^yeet^y l^yih-KAHR-stvuh pah-EH-tuh-moo r^yih-TSEHP-too [s^yih-CHAHS]?

1440. Is it mild?

Оно несильнодействующее?

ah-NOH n^yih-S^yEEL^y-nuh-D^yEH‿EE-stvoo-yoo-shhuh-yuh?

1441. Is it safe?
Оно́ безопа́сно? *ah-NOH bʸih-zah-PAHS-nuh?*

1442. Antibiotic.
Антибио́тик. *ahn-tʸee-bʸee-OH-tʸeek.*

1443. Sleeping pill.
Табле́тка для сна́ (OR: Снотво́рное).
tah-BLʸEHT-kuh dlʸah-SNAH (OR: *snah-TVOHR-nuh-yuh*).

1444. Tranquilizer.
Транквилиза́тор. *truhn-kvʸee-lʸee-ZAH-tuhr.*

1445. Caution.
Осторо́жно. *ah-stah-ROHZH-nuh.*

1446. Poison. Яд. *yaht.*

1447. Take as directed.
Принима́йте как ука́зано.
prʸee-nʸee-MAH‿EE-tʸih kahk oo-KAH-zuh-nuh.

1448. Not to be taken internally.
Не для вну́треннего употребле́ния.
nʸih-dlʸah-VNOO-trʸihn-nʸuh-vuh oo-puh-trʸih-BLʸEH-nʸee-yuh.

1449. For external use only.
То́лько для нару́жного по́льзования.
TOHLʸ-kuh dlʸuh-nah-ROOZH-nuh-vuh POHLʸ-zuh-vuh-nʸee-yuh.

See also "Health and Illness," p. 147.

DRUGSTORE ITEMS

1450. Adhesive tape.
Перевя́зочная ле́нта.
pʸih-rʸih-VʸAH-zuhch-nuh-yuh LʸEHN-tuh.

1451. Alcohol.
Медици́нский спи́рт.
m^yih-d^yee-TSÏN-sk^yee sp^yeert.

1452. Antiseptic.
Антисепти́ческое сре́дство.
ahn-t^yee-sehp-T^yEE-chih-skuh-yuh SR^yEHT-stvuh.

1453. Aspirin (OR: Analgesic).
Аспири́н (OR: Анальги́н).
ah-sp^yee-R^yEEN (OR: ah-nahl^y-G^yEEN).

1454. Band-Aids (bandage with antiseptic adhesive).
Лейкопла́стырь. *l^yih_ee-kuh-PLAH-stïr^y.*

1455. Bandages. Бинты́. *b^yeen-TЇ.*

1456. Bath oil.
Ва́нное ма́сло. *VAHN-nuh-yuh MAHS-luh.*

1457. Bath salts.
Аромати́ческая со́ль для ва́нны.
ah-ruh-mah-T^yEE-chih-skuh-yuh sohl^y dl^yah-VAHN-nï.

1458. Bicarbonate of soda.
Питьева́я со́да. *p^yeet^y-yih-VAH-yuh SOH-duh.*

1459. Bobby pins.
Зако́лки (для воло́с).
zah-KOHL-k^yee (dl^yuh-vah-LOHS).

1460. Boric acid.
Бо́рная кислота́. *BOHR-nuh-yuh k^yees-lah-TAH.*

1461. Chewing gum.
Жева́тельная рези́нка.
zhï-VAH-t^yihl^y-nuh-yuh r^yih-Z^yEEN-kuh.

1462. Cleaning fluid.
Очища́ющая жи́дкость.
ah-chee-SHHAH-yoo-shhuh-yuh ZHЇT-kuhst^y.

1463. Cleansing tissues.
Бума́жные салфе́тки.
boo-MAHZH-nï-yih sahl-F^{y}EHT-k^{y}ee.

1464. Cold cream.
Кре́м для лица́. *kr^{y}ehm dl^{y}uh-l^{y}ee-TSAH.*

1465. Cologne. Одеколо́н. *ah-d^{y}ih-kah-LOHN.*

1466. Comb. Гребёнка. *gr^{y}ih-B^{y}OHN-kuh.*

1467. Contraceptives.
Противозача́точные сре́дства.
pruh-t^{y}ee-vuh-zah-CHAH-tuhch-nï-yih SR^{y}EHT-stvuh.

1468. Corn pad.
Мозо́льный пла́стырь.
mah-ZOHL^y-nï_ee PLAH-stïr^y.

1469. Cotton (absorbent). Ва́та. *VAH-tuh.*

1470. Cough syrup.
Сиро́п от ка́шля. *s^{y}ee-ROHP aht-KAHSH-l^{y}uh.*

1471. Deodorant.
Деодора́нт. *d^{y}ih-ah-dah-RAHNT.*

1472. Depilatory.
Депилато́рий (OR: Сре́дство для удале́ния воло́с).
deh-p^{y}ee-lah-TOH-r^{y}ee (OR: *SR^{y}EHT-stvuh dl^{y}uh-oo-dah-L^{y}EH-n^{y}ee-yuh vah-LOHS.*

1473. Disinfectant.
Дезинфици́рующее сре́дство.
deh-z^{y}een-f^{y}ee-TSÏ-roo-yoo-shhuh-yuh SR^{y}EHT-stvuh.

1474. Ear plugs.
Заглу́шки для уше́й.
zah-GLOOSH-k^{y}ee dl^{y}uh-oo-SHEH_EE.

1475. Enema bag. Кли́зма. *KL^{y}EEZ-muh.*

1476. Epsom salts.
Англи́йская со́ль. *ahn-GL^{y}EE-skuh-yuh sohl^y.*

1477. Eye cup.
Глазна́я ва́нночка. *glahz-NAH-yuh VAHN-nuhch-kuh.*

1478. Eye wash.
Глазна́я примо́чка.
glahz-NAH-yuh pr^yee-MOHCH-kuh.

1479. Gauze. Ма́рля. *MAHR-l^yuh.*

1480. Hairbrush.
Щётка для воло́с. *SHHOHT-kuh dl^yuh-vah-LOHS.*

1481. Hair clip.
Зажи́м для воло́с. *zah-ZHЇM dl^yuh-vah-LOHS.*

1482. Hair net.
Се́тка для воло́с. *S^yEHT-kuh dl^yuh-vah-LOHS.*

1483. Hairpins. Шпи́льки. *SHP^yEEL^y-k^yee.*

1484. Hairspray.
Ла́к для воло́с. *lahk dl^yuh-vah-LOHS.*

1485. Hand lotion.
Лосьо́н для рук. *lahs^y-YOHN dl^yah-ROOK.*

1486. Hot-water bottle. Гре́лка. *GR^yEHL-kuh.*

1487. Ice bag.
Пузы́рь со льдо́м. *poo-ZЇR^y sahl^y-DOHM.*

1488. Insecticide.
Сре́дство от насеко́мых.
SR^yEHT-stvuh aht-nuh-s^yih-KOH-mïkh.

1489. Iodine. Йо́д. *yoht.*

1490. Laxative (mild).
(Несильноде́йствующее) слаби́тельное.
(n^yih-S^yEEL^y-nuh-D^yEH_EE-stvoo-yoo-shhuh-yuh)
slah-B^yEE-t^yihl^y-nuh-yuh.

1491. Lipstick.
Губна́я пома́да. *goob-NAH-yuh pah-MAH-duh.*

1492. Medicine dropper. Пипе́тка. *p^yee-P^yEHT-kuh.*

1493. Mirror. Зе́ркало. *Z^yEHR-kuh-luh.*

1494. Mouthwash.
Полоска́ние для рта́.
puh-lah-SKAH-n^yee-yuh dl^yahr-TAH.

1495. Nail file.
Пи́лка для ногте́й.
P^yEEL-kuh dl^yuh-nahk-T^yEH⌣EE.

1496. Nail polish.
Ла́к для ногте́й. *lahk dl^yuh-nahk-T^yEH⌣EE.*

1497. Nose drops.
Носовы́е ка́пли. *nuh-sah-VĬ-yih KAH-pl^yee.*

1498. Ointment. Ма́зь. *mahs^y.*

1499. Peroxide.
Пе́рекись водоро́да.
P^yEH-r^yih-k^yees^y vuh-dah-ROH-duh.

1500. Powder. Порошо́к. *puh-rah-SHOHK.*

1501. Face powder.
Пу́дра для лица́. *POO-druh dl^yuh-l^yee-TSAH.*

1502. Foot powder.
Пу́дра для но́г. *POO-druh dl^yah-NOHK.*

1503. Talcum powder. Та́льк. *tahl^yk.*

1504. Powder puff. Пухо́вка. *poo-KHOHF-kuh.*

1505. Straight razor.
Опа́сная бри́тва. *ah-PAHS-nuh-yuh BR^yEET-vuh.*

1506. Electric razor.
Электри́ческая бри́тва.
eh-l^yihk-TR^yEE-chih-skuh-yuh BR^yEET-vuh.

1507. Safety razor.
Безопа́сная бри́тва.
b^yih-zah-PAHS-nuh-yuh BR^yEET-vuh.

1508. Razor blade.
Ле́звие для бри́твы.
L^yEHZ-v^yee-yuh dl^yah-BR^yEET-vï.

1509. Rouge. Румя́на. *roo-M^yAH-nuh.*

1510. Sanitary napkins.
Гигиени́ческие поду́шечки.
*g^yee-g^yee-yih-N^yEE-chih-sk^yee-yih
pah-DOO-shuhch-k^yee.*

1511. Sedative.
Успока́ивающее сре́дство.
oo-spah-KAH-yee-vuh-yoo-shhuh-yuh SR^yEHT-stvuh.

1512. Shampoo. Шампу́нь. *shahm-POON^y.*

1513. Shaving brush.
Ки́сточка для бритья́.
K^yEE-stuhch-kuh dl^yuh-br^yeet^y-YAH.

1514. Shaving cream (brushless).
Кре́м для бритья́. *kr^yehm dl^yuh-br^yeet^y-YAH.*

1515. Shaving lotion.
Лосьо́н для бритья́. *lahs^y-YOHN dl^yuh-br^yeet^y-YAH.*

1516. Shower cap.
Ша́почка для ду́ша.
SHAH-puhch-kuh dl^yah-DOO-shuh.

1517. Smelling salts.
Ню́хательная со́ль.
N^yOO-khuh-t^yihl^y-nuh-yuh sohl^y.

1518. Sponge. Гу́бка. *GOOP-kuh.*

1519. Sunburn ointment.
Мазь от солнечного ожога.
mahs^y aht-SOHL-n^{y}ihch-nuh-vuh ah-ZHOH-guh.

1520. Sunglasses.
Защитные очки от солнца.
zah-SHHEET-nï-yih ahch-K^{y}EE aht-SOHN-tsuh.

1521. Suntan oil (OR: lotion).
Мазь (OR: Лосьон) для загара.
mahs^y (OR: lahs^y-YOHN) dl^{y}uh-zah-GAH-ruh.

1522. Syringe. Шприц. *shpr^{y}eets.*

1523. Tampons. Тампоны. *tahm-POH-nï.*

1524. Thermometer [Celsius] [Fahrenheit].
Термометр [Цельсия] [Фаренгейта].
t^{y}ihr-MOH-m^{y}ih-tuhr [TSEHL^y-s^{y}ee-yuh]
[fuh-r^{y}ihn-G^{y}EH ‿ EE-tuh].

1525. Toothbrush.
Зубная щётка. *zoob-NAH-yuh SHHOT-kuh.*

1526. Toothpaste.
Зубная паста. *zoob-NAH-yuh PAH-stuh.*

1527. Tooth powder.
Зубной порошок. *zoob-NOY puh-rah-SHOHK.*

1528. Vaseline. Вазелин. *vuh-z^{y}ih-L^{y}EEN.*

1529. Vitamins. Витамины. *v^{y}ee-tah-M^{y}EE-nï.*

CAMERA SHOP AND PHOTOGRAPHY

1530. I want a roll of film [for this camera].
Я хочу плёнку [для этого фотоаппарата].
yah khah-CHOO PL^{y}OHN-koo [dl^{y}ah-EH-tuh-vuh
FOH-tah-ah-pah-RAH-tuh].

1531. Do you have [color film]?

У вас есть [цветная плёнка]?

oo-VAHS yehst^y [tsv^{y}iht-NAH-yuh PL^{y}OHN-kuh]?

1532. —black-and-white film.

—чёрно-белая плёнка.

—CHOHR-nuh –B^{y}EH-luh-yuh PL^{y}OHN-kuh.

1533. —movie film.

—киноплёнка.   *—k^{y}ee-nah-PL^{y}OHN-kuh.*

1534. What is the charge [for developing a roll]?

Сколько стоит [проявка одной катушки]?

SKOHL^y-kuh STOH-yiht [prah-YAHF-kuh ahd-NOY kah-TOOSH-k^{y}ee]?

1535. —for enlarging.

—увеличение.   *—oo-v^{y}ih-l^{y}ee-CHEH-n^{y}ee-yuh.*

1536. —for one print.

—один отпечаток.

—ah-D^{y}EEN aht-p^{y}ih-CHAH-tuhk.

1537. May I take a photo of you?

Позвольте вас сфотографировать.

pah-ZVOHL^y-t^{y}ih vahs sfuh-tuh-grah-F^{y}EE-ruh-vuht^y

1538. Would you take a photo of [me] [us], please?

Сфотографируйте [меня] [нас], пожалуйста.

sfuh-tuh-grah-F^{y}EE-roo_ee-t^{y}ih [m^{y}ih-N^{y}AH] [nahs], pah-ZHAH-lï-stuh.

1539. A color print.

Цветной отпечаток.

tsv^{y}iht-NOY aht-p^{y}ih-CHAH-tuhk.

1540. Flashbulb.

Лампа для вспышки.

LAHM-puh dl^{y}ah-FSPÏSH-k^{y}ee.

1541. The lens.   Объектив.   *ahb-yihk-T^{y}EEF.*

1542. The negative. Негати́в. *n^yih-gah-T^yEEF.*

1543. The shutter. Затво́р. *zah-TVOHR.*

1544. A transparency (OR: **slide**).
Диапозити́в (OR: Сла́йд).
d^yee-uh-puh-z^yee-T^yEEF (OR: *slah͡_eet*).

1545. A tripod.
Трено́жник. *tr^yih-NOHZH-n^yeek.*

See also "Repairs and Adjustments," p. 134.

GIFTS AND SOUVENIRS

1546. Amber. Янта́рь. *yihn-TAHR^y.*

1547. Basket. Корзи́нка. *kahr-Z^yEEN-kuh.*

1548. Box of candy.
Коро́бка конфе́т. *kah-ROHP-kuh kahn-F^yEHT.*

1549. Doll. Ку́кла. *KOO-kluh.*

1550. Embroidery. Вы́шивка. *VĬ-shĭf-kuh.*

1551. Fur hats.
Мехов́ые ша́пки. *m^yih-khah-VĬ-yih SHAHP-k^yee.*

1552. Handicrafts.
Ручна́я рабо́та. *rooch-NAH-yuh rah-BOH-tuh.*

1553. Jewelry.
Ювели́рные изде́лия.
yoo-v^yih-L^yEER-nĭ-yih eez-D^yEH-l^yee-yuh.

1554. Knitting. Вяза́ние. *v^yih-ZAH-n^yee-yuh.*

1555. Lace. Кружева́. *kroo-zhĭ-VAH.*

1556. Matryoshka doll.*
Матрёшка. *mah-TR^yOHSH-kuh.*

---

* A nested set of painted wooden dolls depicting a woman
dressed in Russian costume.

1557. Penknife.
Перочинный нож. *p^yih-rah-CHEEN-nï__ee nohsh.*

1558. Perfume. Духи. *doo-KH^yEE.*

1559. Phonograph records.
Грампластинки. *gruhm-plah-ST^yEEN-k^yee.*

1560. Pottery. Керамика. *k^yih-RAH-m^yee-kuh.*

1561. Precious stone.
Драгоценная камень.
druh-gah-TSEHN-nuh-yuh KAH-m^yihn^y.

1562. Print (graphic).
Эстамп (OR: Графика).
eh-STAHMP (OR: GRAH-f^yee-kuh).

1563. Reproduction (of painting, etc.).
Репродукция. *r^yih-prah-DOOK-tsï-yuh.*

1564. Samovar. Самовар. *suh-mah-VAHR.*

1565. Souvenir. Сувенир. *soo-v^yih-N^yEER.*

1566. Toys. Игрушки. *ee-GROOSH-k^yee.*

TOBACCO STORE

1567. Where is the nearest tobacco store?
Где ближайший табачный магазин?
*gd^yeh bl^yee-ZHAH__EE-shï__ee tah-BAHCH-nï__ee
    muh-gah-Z^yEEN?*

1568. I want some cigars.
Я хочу сигары. *yah khah-CHOO s^yee-GAH-rï.*

1569. What brands of American cigarettes [with menthol] do you have?

Какие у вас марки американских сигарет [с ментолом]?

kah-K^yEE-yih oo-VAHS MAHR-k^yee ah-m^yih-r^yee-KAHN-sk^yeekh s^yee-gah-R^yEHT [sm^yihn-TOH-luhm]?

1570. One pack of king-size [filter-tip] cigarettes.

Одну пачку длинных сигарет [с фильтром].

ahd-NOO PAHCH-koo DL^yEEN-nïkh s^yee-gah-R^yEHT [SF^yEEL^y-truhm].

1571. I need a lighter.

Мне нужна зажигалка.

mn^yeh noozh-NAH zuh-zhï-GAHL-kuh.

1572. Lighter fluid.

Бензин для зажигалки.

b^yihn-Z^yEEN dl^yuh-zuh-zhï-GAHL-k^yee.

1573. Flint. Кремень. *kr^yih-M^yEHN^y.*

1574. Matches. Спички. *SP^yEECH-k^yee.*

1575. A pipe. Трубка. *TROOP-kuh.*

1576. Pipe cleaners.

Щёточки для трубки.

SHHOH-tuhch-k^yee dl^yah-TROOP-k^yee.

1577. Pipe tobacco.

Трубочный табак. *TROO-buhch-nï＿ee tah-BAHK.*

1578. Russian cigarettes (with hollow cardboard mouthpiece).

Папиросы. *puh-p^yee-ROH-sï.*

1579. Tobacco pouch. Кисет. *k^yee-S^yEHT.*

LAUNDRY AND DRY CLEANING

1580. Where can I take my laundry to be washed?
Куда отдать бельё в стирку?
koo-DAH ahd-DAHT *b* *ih* *l* *-YOH FST* *EER-koo?*

1581. Is there a dry-cleaning service near here?
Есть химчистка недалеко отсюда?
yehst *kh* *eem-CHEEST-kuh n* *ih-duh-l* *ih-KOH
aht-S* *OO-duh?*

1582. Wash this blouse [in hot water].
Стирайте эту блузку [в горячей воде].
st *ee-RAH ͜ EE-t* *ih EH-too BLOOS-koo
[vgah-R* *AH-chih ͜ ee vah-D* *EH].*

1583. —in warm water.
—в тёплой воде.   —*FT* *OH-pluh ͜ ee vah-D* *EH.*

1584. —in lukewarm water.
—в тепловатой воде.
—*ft* *ih-plah-VAH-tuh ͜ ee vah-D* *EH.*

1585. —in cold water.
—в холодной воде.
—*ʃkhah-LOHD-nuh ͜ ee vah-D* *EH.*

1586. No starch, please.
Прошу не крахмалить.
prah-SHOO n *ih-krahkh-MAH-l* *eet* *.*

1587. Remove the stain [from this shirt].
Удалите пятно [с этой рубашки].
oo-dah-L *EE-t* *ih p* *iht-NOH [SEH-tuh ͜ ee roo-BAHSH-
k* *ee].*

1588. Press [the trousers].
Выгладите [брюки].
VĬ-gluh-d *ee-t* *ih [BR* *OO-k* *ee].*

1589. Starch [the collar].

Покрахма́льте [воротни́к].

puh-krahkh-MAHL^y-t^yih [vuh-raht-N^yEEK].

1590. Dry clean [this coat].

Вы́чистите химчи́сткой [э́то пальто́].

*VǏ-chee-st^yee-t^yih kh^yeem-CHEEST-kuh ̶ee
 [EH-tuh pahl^y-TOH].*

1591. [The belt] is missing.

Не хвата́ет [по́яса].

n^yih-khvah-TAH-yiht [POH-yih-suh].

1592. Sew on [this button].

Пришье́йте [э́ту пу́говицу].

pr^yee-SHEH ̶EE-t^yih [EH-too POO-guh-v^yee-tsoo].

See also "Repairs and Adjustments".

REPAIRS AND ADJUSTMENTS

1593. This does not work.

Э́то не рабо́тает. *EH-tuh n^yih-rah-BOH-tuh-yiht.*

1594. This watch [is fast] [is slow].

Э́ти часы́ [спеша́т] [отстаю́т].

EH-t^yee chih-SǏ [sp^yih-SHAHT] [aht-stah-YOOT].

1595. [My glasses] are broken.

[Мой очки́] сло́маны.

[mah-YEE ahch-K^yEE] SLOH-muh-nï.

1596. This is torn.

Э́то по́рвано. *EH-tuh POHR-vuh-nuh.*

1597. Where can I get this repaired?

Где мо́жно э́то почини́ть?

gd^yeh MOHZH-nuh EH-tuh puh-chee-N^yEET^y?

1598. Fix [this lock].
Почини́те [э́тот замо́к].
puh-chee-N^{y}EE-t^{y}ih [EH-tuht zah-MOHK].

1599. —the sole. —подо́шву. —*pah-DOHSH-voo.*

1600. —the heel. —каблу́к. —*kah-BLOOK.*

1601. —the uppers.
—ве́рхнюю ча́сть боти́нка.
—*V^{y}EHRKH-n^{y}oo-yoo chahst^y bah-T^{y}EEN-kuh.*

1602. —the strap.
—ремешо́к. —*r^{y}ih-m^{y}ih-SHOHK.*

1603. Adjust [this hearing aid].
Отрегули́руйте [э́тот слухово́й аппара́т].
aht-r^{y}ih-goo-L^{y}EE-roo͜_ee-t^{y}ih [EH-tuht sloo-khah-VOY ah-pah-RAHT].

1604. Lengthen [this skirt].
Удлини́те [э́ту ю́бку].
oo-dl^{y}ee-N^{y}EE-t^{y}ih [EH-too YOOP-koo].

1605. Shorten [the sleeves].
Укороти́те [рукава́].
oo-kuh-rah-T^{y}EE-t^{y}ih [roo-kah-VAH].

1606. Replace [the lining].
Замени́те [подкла́дку].
zuh-m^{y}ih-N^{y}EE-t^{y}ih [paht-KLAHT-koo].

1607. Mend [the pocket].
Заштопайте [карма́н].
zah-SHTOH-puh͜_ee-t^{y}ih [kahr-MAHN].

1608. Fasten this together.
Скрепи́те э́то. *skr^{y}ih-P^{y}EE-t^{y}ih EH-tuh.*

1609. Clean [the mechanism].
Почи́стите механи́зм.
pah-CHEE-st^{y}ee-t^{y}ih m^{y}ih-khah-N^{y}EE-zuhm.

1610. Lubricate [the spring].
Смажьте пружину. *SMAHSH-t^{y}ih proo-ZHĬ-noo.*

1611. Needle. Иголка. *ee-GOHL-kuh.*

1612. Scissors. Ножницы. *NOHZH-n^{y}ee-tsĭ.*

1613. Thimble. Напёрсток. *nah-P^{y}OHR-stuhk.*

1614. Thread. Нитка. *N^{y}EET-kuh.*

BARBER SHOP

1615. A haircut, please.
Постригите меня, пожалуйста.
puh-str^{y}ee-G^{y}EE-t^{y}ih m^{y}ih-N^{y}AH, pah-ZHAH-lĭ-stuh.

1616. Just a trim.
Только подстригите меня.
TOHL^y-kuh puht-str^{y}ee-G^{y}EE-t^{y}ih m^{y}ih-N^{y}AH.

1617. A shave.
Побрейте меня. *pah-BR^{y}EH＿EE-t^{y}ih m^{y}ih-N^{y}AH.*

1618. A shoeshine.
Почистите ботинки.
pah-CHEE-st^{y}ee-t^{y}ih bah-T^{y}EEN-k^{y}ee.

1619. Don't cut much [off the top].
Не подстригайте слишком [с верху].
n^{y}ih-puht-str^{y}ih-GAH＿EE-t^{y}ih SL^{y}EESH-kuhm [SV^{y}EHR-khoo].

1620. —off the sides. —с боков. *—zbah-KOHF.*

1621. I want to keep my hair long.
Я хочу оставить волосы длинными.
yah khah-CHOO ah-STAH-v^{y}eet^y VOH-luh-sĭ DL^{y}EEN-nĭ-m^{y}ee.

1622. I part my hair [on this side].
Я делаю себе пробор [с этой стороны].
yah DʸEH-luh-yoo sʸih-BʸEH prah-BOHR [SEH-tuh＿ee stuh-rah-NЇ].

1623. —on the other side.
—с другой стороны. *—zdroo-GOY stuh-rah-NЇ.*

1624. —in the middle.
—в середине. *—fsʸih-rʸih-DʸEE-nʸih.*

1625. Trim [my mustache].
Подстригите [мои усы].
puht-strʸee-GʸEE-tʸih [mah-YEE oo-SЇ].

1626. —my eyebrows.
—мои брови. *—mah-YEE BROH-vʸee.*

1627. —my beard.
—мою бороду. *—mah-YOO BOH-ruh-doo.*

1628. —my sideburns.
—мои бачки. *—mah-YEE BAHCH-kʸee.*

BEAUTY PARLOR

1629. Can I make an appointment for [Monday afternoon]?
Вы можете записать меня на [понедельник днём]?
vї MOH-zhuh-tʸih zuh-pʸee-SAHTʸ mʸih-NʸAH nuh-[puh-nʸih-DʸEHLʸ-nʸeek dnʸohm]?

1630. Comb my hair.
Причешите меня. *prʸee-chih-SHЇ-tʸih mʸih-NʸAH.*

1631. Wash my hair.
Вымойте волосы. *VЇ-muh＿ee-tʸih VOH-luh-sї.*

1632. Blow-dry my hair.
Уложи́те мне во́лосы фе́ном.
oo-lah-ZHĬ-tᵞih mnᵞeh VOH-luh-sï FᵞEH-nuhm.

1633. Shampoo and set, please.
Вы́мойте и уложи́те во́лосы, пожа́луйста.
VĬ-muh ̮ee-tᵞih ee oo-lah-ZHĬ-tᵞih VOH-luh-sï,
pah-ZHAH-lï-stuh.

1634. Not too short.
Не сли́шком ко́ротко.
nᵞih-SLᵞEESH-kuhm KOH-ruht-kuh.

1635. In this style, please.
По э́тому фасо́ну, пожа́луйста.
pah-EH-tuh-moo fah-SOH-noo, pah-ZHAH-lï-stuh.

1636. Dye my hair [in this shade].
Покра́сьте во́лосы [в э́тот цвет].
pah-KRAHSᵞ-tᵞih VOH-luh-sï [VEH-tuht tsvᵞeht].

1637. Clean and set this wig.
Вы́мойте и уложи́те э́тот пари́к.
VĬ-muh ̮ee-tᵞih ee oo-lah-ZHĬ-tᵞih EH-tuht pah-RᵞEEK.

1638. A curl. Зави́вка. *zah-VᵞEEF-kuh.*

1639. A facial.
Очище́ние и масса́ж лица́.
ah-chee-SHHHEH-nᵞee-yuh ee mah-SAHSH lᵞee-TSAH.

1640. A hair-dryer. Фе́н. *fᵞehn.*

1641. A hairpiece. Накла́дка. *nah-KLAHT-kuh.*

1642. A manicure. Маникю́р. *muh-nᵞee-KᵞOOR.*

1643. A massage. Масса́ж. *mah-SAHSH.*

1644. A permanent wave.
Пермане́нт. *pᵞihr-mah-NᵞEHNT.*

STORES AND SERVICES

1645. Antique shop.
Антиква́рный магази́н.
*ahn-t*ᵞ*ee-KVAHR-nï_ee muh-gah-Z*ᵞ*EEN.*

1646. Art gallery.
Карти́нная галлере́я.
*kahr-T*ᵞ*EEN-nuh-yuh guh-l*ᵞ*ih-R*ᵞ*EH-yuh.*

1647. Artist's materials.
Принадле́жности худо́жника.
*pr*ᵞ*ee-nahd-L*ᵞ*EHZH-nuh-st*ᵞ*ee khoo-DOHZH-n*ᵞ*ee-kuh.*

1648. Auto rental.
Аре́нда автомоби́ля.
*ah-R*ᵞ*EHN-duh ahf-tuh-mah-B*ᵞ*EE-l*ᵞ*uh.*

1649. Auto repairs.
Авторемо́нтная мастерска́я.
*ahf-tuh-r*ᵞ*ih-MOHNT-nuh-yuh muh-st*ᵞ*ihr-SKAH-yuh.*

1650. Bakery. Бу́лочная. *BOO-luhch-nuh-yuh.*

1651. Bank. Ба́нк. *bahnk.*

1652. Bar. Ба́р. *bahr.*

1653. Barber.
Парикма́херская. *puh-r*ᵞ*eek-MAH-kh*ᵞ*ihr-skuh-yuh.*

1654. Beauty parlor (OR: **Ladies' hairdresser**).
Да́мский сало́н. *DAHM-sk*ᵞ*ee sah-LOHN.*

1655. Beryozka (store selling goods to foreigners for hard currency).
Берёзка. *b*ᵞ*ih-R*ᵞ*OHS-kuh.*

1656. Bookshop.
Кни́ги (OR: Кни́жный магази́н).
*KN*ᵞ*EE-g*ᵞ*ee* (OR: *KN*ᵞ*EEZH-nï_ee muh-gah-Z*ᵞ*EEN*).

1657. Butcher.
Мя́со (OR: Мясни́к).   *M^yAH-suh* (OR: *m^yihs-N^yEEK*).

1658. Candy shop.
Конди́терская.   *kahn-D^yEE-t^yihr-skuh-yuh.*

1659. Clothing store.
Оде́жда (OR: Магази́н оде́жды).
ah-D^yEHZH-duh (OR: *muh-gah-Z^yEEN ah-D^yEHZH-dï*).

1660. Children's clothing store.
Де́тская оде́жда (OR: Магази́н де́тской оде́жды).
D^yEHT-skuh-yuh ah-D^yEHZH-duh (OR: *muh-gah-Z^yEEN
D^yEHT-skuh_ee ah-D^yEHZH-dï*).

1661. Men's clothing store.
Мужска́я оде́жда (OR: Магази́н мужско́й оде́жды).
moosh-SKAH-yuh ah-D^yEHZH-duh (OR:
muh-gah-Z^yEEN moosh-SKOY ah-D^yEHZH-dï).

1662. Ladies' clothing store.
Да́мская оде́жда (OR: Магази́н да́мской оде́жды).
DAHM-skuh-yuh ah-D^yEHZH-duh (OR:
muh-gah-Z^yEEN DAHM-skuh_ee ah-D^yEHZH-dï).

1663. Cosmetics.
Косме́тика.   *kahs-M^yEH-t^yee-kuh.*

1664. Dairy products. Молоко́.   *muh-lah-KOH.*

1665. Dance studio.
Танцева́льная сту́дия.
tuhn-tsï-VAHL^y-nuh-yuh STOO-d^yee-yuh.

1666. Delicatessen.
Гастроно́м.   *guh-strah-NOHM.*

1667. Dentist. Зубно́й вра́ч.   *zoob-NOY vrahch.*

1668. Department store.
Универма́г.   *oo-n^yee-v^yihr-MAHK.*

1669. Dressmaker. Ателье́. *ah-t^{y}ihl^y-YEH.*

1670. Drugstore (OR: **Pharmacy**).
Апте́ка. *ahp-T^{y}EH-kuh.*

1671. Dry foods.
Бакале́я. *buh-kah-L^{y}EH-yuh.*

1672. Drycleaners.
Химчи́стка. *kh^{y}eem-CHEEST-kuh.*

1673. Electrical supplies.
Электротова́ры (OR: Электроприбо́ры, OR: Свет).
eh-L^{y}EHK-truh-tah-VAH-rï (OR: *eh-L^{y}EHK-truh-pr^{y}ee-BOH-rï,* OR: *sv^{y}eht*).

1674. Fabric store. Тка́ни. *TKAH-n^{y}ee.*

1675. Fish store. Ры́ба. *RÏ-buh.*

1676. Florist.
Цветы́ (OR: Цвето́чный магази́н).
tsv^{y}ih-TÏ (OR: *tsv^{y}ih-TOHCH-nï_ee muh-gah-Z^{y}EEN*).

1677. Fruit store.
Фру́кты (OR: Óвощи-фру́кты).
FROOK-tï (OR: *OH-vuh-shhee-FROOK-tï*).

1678. Funeral parlor.
Похоро́нное бюро́.
puh-khah-ROHN-nuh-yuh b^{y}oo-ROH.

1679. Furniture store.
Ме́бель. *M^{y}EH-b^{y}ihl^y.*

1680. Gift store. Пода́рки. *pah-DAHR-k^{y}ee.*

1681. Grocery.
Гастроно́м (OR: Продово́льственный магази́н).
guh-strah-NOHM (OR: *pruh-dah-VOHL^y-stv^{y}ihn-nï_ee muh-gah-Z^{y}EEN*).

1682. Men's hairdresser.
Мужска́я парикма́херская.
moosh-SKAH-yuh puh-r^{y}eek-MAH-kh^{y}ihr-skuh-yuh.

1683. Hardware store.
Строи́тельные материа́лы.
strah-YEE-t^{y}ihl^y-nï-yih muh-t^{y}ih-r^{y}ee-AH-lï.

1684. Hat shop.
Головны́е убо́ры. *guh-lahv-N$Ï$-yih oo-BOH-rï.*

1685. Housewares.
Хозя́йственные това́ры.
khah-Z^{y}AH＿EE-stv^{y}ihn-nï-yih tah-VAH-rï.

1686. Jewelry store.
Ювели́рные изде́лия.
yoo-v^{y}ih-L^{y}EER-nï-yih eez-D^{y}EH-l^{y}ee-yuh.

1687. Lawyer. Адвока́т. *ahd-vah-KAHT.*

1688. Laundry.
Пра́чечная. *PRAH-chihch-nuh-yuh.*

1689. Lumberyard.
Де́рево (OR: Лесоматериа́л, OR: Лесно́й скла́д).
D^{y}EH-r^{y}ih-vuh (OR: *l^{y}ih-suh-muh-t^{y}ih-r^{y}ee-AHL,*
OR: *l^{y}ihs-NOY sklaht).*

1690. Market. Ры́нок. *R$Ï$-nuhk.*

1691. Milliner. Моди́стка. *mah-D^{y}EEST-kuh.*

1692. Money exchange.
Обме́н валю́той. *ahb-M^{y}EHN vah-L^{y}OO-tuh＿ee.*

1693. Music store. Но́ты. *NOH-tï.*

1694. Musical instruments.
Музыка́льные инструме́нты.
moo-zï-KAHL^y-nï-yih een-stroo-M^{y}EHN-tï.

1695. Newsstand.
Газе́ты (OR: Союзпеча́ть, OR: Газе́тный кио́ск).
gah-Z^yEH-tï (OR: sah-YOOS-p^yih-CHAHT^y, OR: gah-Z^yEHT-nï_ee k^yee-OHSK).

1696. Paints. Кра́ски. *KRAHS-k^yee.*

1697. Pastry shop (LIT.: **Confectionery**).
Конди́терская. *kahn-D^yEE-t^yihr-skuh-yuh.*

1698. Perfume shop.
Духи́ (OR: Парфюме́рия).
doo-KH^yEE (OR: puhr-f^yoo-M^yEH-r^yee-yuh).

1699. Pet shop.
Зоомагази́н. *zah-ah-muh-gah-Z^yEEN.*

1700. Photographer.
Фо́тоателье́ (OR: Фотогра́фия).
FOH-tah-ah-t^yihl^y-YEH (OR: fuh-tah-GRAH-f^yee-yuh).

1701. Sausage store. Колба́сы. *kahl-BAH-sï.*

1702. Secondhand store.
Комиссио́нный магази́н.
kuh-m^yee-s^yee-OHN-nï_ee muh-gah-Z^yEEN.

1703. Sewing machine.
Швейная маши́на.
SHV^yEH_EE-nuh-yuh mah-SHÏ-nuh.

1704. Shoemaker. Сапо́жник. *sah-POHZH-n^yeek.*

1705. Shoe store. О́бувь. *OH-boof^y*

1706. Sightseeing.
Осмо́тр достопримеча́тельностей.
ah-SMOH-tuhr duh-stuh-pr^yee-m^yih-CHAH-t^yihl^y-nuh-st^yih_ee.

1707. Sporting goods.
Спорти́вные принадле́жности.
spahr-T^yEEV-nï-yih pr^yee-nahd-L^yEHZH-nuh-st^yee.

1708. Stockbroker.
Биржевóй мáклер.
b^yeer-zhï-VOY MAH-kl^yihr.

1709. Supermarket.
Универсáм. *oo-n^yee-v^yihr-SAHM.*

1710. Tailor. Портнóй. *pahrt-NOY.*

1711. Tobacco shop.
Папирóсы–сигарéты–табáк (OR: Табáк, OR:
    Табáчный магазúн).
puh-p^yee-ROH-sï–s^yee-gah-R^yEH-tï–tah-BAHK
    (OR: *tah-BAHK,* OR: *tah-BAHCH-nï_ee*
    muh-gah-Z^yEEN).

1712. Toy shop. Игрýшки. *ee-GROOSH-k^yee.*

1713. Trucking.
Перевóзка грýзов. *p^yih-r^yih-VOHS-kuh GROO-zuhf.*

1714. Upholsterer.
Драпирóвщик. *druh-p^yee-ROHF-shheek.*

1715. Used cars.
Подéржанные автомобúли.
pah-D^yEHR-zhuhn-nï-yih ahf-tuh-mah-B^yEE-l^yee.

1716. Vegetable store.
Óвощи (OR: Óвощи — фрýкты).
OH-vuh-shhee (OR: *OH-vuh-shhee-FROOK-tï*).

1717. Watchmaker.
Часовщúк (OR: Часы́).
chih-sahf-SHHEEK (OR: *chih-SЇ*).

1718. Wines and liquors.
Вúна.* *V^yEE-nuh.*

---

* Stores marked Консéрвы (*kahn-S^yEHR-vï,* "bottled and canned goods") also carry wines and liquors.

BABY CARE

1719. I need a reliable babysitter tonight [at 7 o'clock].

Мне нужна надёжная няня для ребёнка сегодня вечером [в семь часов].

mn^yeh noozh-NAH nah-D^yOHZH-nuh-yuh N^yAH-n^yuh dl^yuh-r^yih-B^yOHN-kuh s^yih-VOHD-n^yuh V^yEH-chih-ruhm [fs^yehm^y chih-SOHF].

1720. Call a pediatrician immediately.

Вызовите детского врача сейчас же.

VĬ-zuh-v^yee-t^yih D^yEHT-skuh-vuh vrah-CHAH s^yih-CHAHZH-zhuh.

1721. Feed the baby.

Накормите ребёнка.

nuh-kahr-M^yEE-t^yih r^yih-B^yOHN-kuh.

1722. Change the diaper.

Перемените пелёнки.

p^yih-r^yih-m^yih-N^yEE-t^yih p^yih-L^yOHN-k^yee.

1723. Bathe the baby.

Выкупайте ребёнка.

VĬ-koo-puh＿ee-t^yih r^yih-B^yOHN-kuh.

1724. Put the baby in the crib for a nap.

Положите ребёнка в кроватку спать.

puh-lah-ZHĬ-t^yih r^yih-B^yOHN-kuh fkrah-VAHT-koo spaht^y.

1725. Give the baby a pacifier if it cries.

Давайте ребёнку пустышку, если он будет плакать.

dah-VAH＿EE-t^yih r^yih-B^yOHN-koo poo-STĬSH-koo, YEHS-l^yee ohn BOO-d^yiht PLAH-kuht^y.

1726. Do you have an ointment for diaper rash?

Есть у вас мазь от сыпи для грудного ребёнка?

yehst^y oo-VAHS mahs^y aht-SĬ-p^yee dl^yuh-grood-NOH-vuh r^yih-B^yOHN-kuh?

1727. Take the baby to the park [in the carriage].
Отвезите ребёнка в парк [в коляске].
aht-vʸih-ZʸEE-tʸih rʸih-BʸOHN-kuh fpahrk
  [ʃkah-LʸAHS-kʸih].

1728. —in the stroller.
—в прогулочной коляске.
—*fprah-GOO-luhch-nuh__ee kah-LʸAHS-kʸih.*

1729. Baby (OR: Strained) food.
Детское (OR: Протёртое) питание.
DʸEHT-skuh-yuh (OR: *prah-TʸOHR-tuh-yuh*)
  pʸee-TAH-nʸee-yuh.

1730. Baby powder.
Детский порошок. *DʸEHT-skʸee puh-rah-SHOHK.*

1731. Bib.
Нагрудник (OR: Слюнявчик).
nah-GROOD-nʸeek (OR: *slʸoo-NʸAHF-cheek*).

1732. Colic. Колики. *KOH-lʸee-kʸee.*

1733. Disposable bottles.
Бутылки разового пользования.
boo-TĬL-kʸee RAH-zuh-vuh-vuh POHLʸ-zuh-vuh-
  nʸee-yuh.

1734. Disposable diapers.
Бумажные пелёнки.
boo-MAHZH-nĭ-yih pʸih-LʸOHN-kʸee.

1735. High chair.
Высокий стульчик (для ребёнка).
vĭ-SOH-kʸee STOOLʸ-cheek (*dlʸuh-rʸih-BʸOHN-kuh*).

1736. Nursemaid. Няня. *NʸAH-nʸuh.*

1737. Playground.
Спортивная площадка.
spahr-TʸEEV-nuh-yuh plah-SHHAHT-kuh.

1738. Playpen.
Детский манеж. *D*^y*EHT-sk*^y*ee mah-N*^y*EHSH.*

1739. Rattle.
Погремушка. *puh-gr*^y*ih-MOOSH-kuh.*

1740. Stuffed toy.
Мягкая игрушка.
M^y*AHKH-kuh-yuh ee-GROOSH-kuh.*

HEALTH AND ILLNESS

1741. Is the doctor [at home] [in his office]?
Доктор [дома] [в своём кабинете]?
DOHK-tuhr [DOH-muh] [fsvah-YOHM
kuh-b^y*ee-N*^y*EH-t*^y*ih]?*

1742. What are his office hours?
Какие его приёмные часы?
kah-K^y*EE-yih yih-VOH pr*^y*ee-YOHM-nï-yih chih-SÏ?*

1743. Take my temperature.
Измерьте мне температуру.
eez-M^y*EHR*^y*-t*^y*ih mn*^y*eh t*^y*ihm-p*^y*ih-rah-TOO-roo.*

1744. I have something [in my eye].
Что-то попало мне [в глаз].
SHTOH-tuh pah-PAH-luh mn^y*eh [vglahs].*

1745. I have a pain [in my back].
У меня болит [спина].*
oo-m^y*ih-N*^y*AH bah-L*^y*EET [sp*^y*ee-NAH].*

---

* This phrase is used for most aches and pains in Russian.
Thus, "I have a sore [throat]" is usually translated "У меня
болит [горло]" (*oo-m*^y*ih-N*^y*AH bah-L*^y*EET [GOHR-luh]*);
words for other parts of the body may be substituted.

1746. —in my shoulder. —плечо́. —*pl^yih-CHOH.*

1747. My head hurts (OR: I have a headache).
У меня́ боли́т голова́.*
oo-m^yih-N^yAH bah-L^yEET guh-lah-VAH.

1748. [My toe] is swollen.
[Мой па́лец ноги́] опу́х.
[*moy PAH-l^yihts nah-G^yEE*] *ah-POOKH.*

1749. It is sensitive to pressure.
Он чувстви́телен к прикоснове́нию.
ohn choost-V^yEE-t^yih-l^yihn kpr^yee-kuhs-nah-V^yEH-n^yee-yoo.

1750. Is it serious?
Э́то серьёзно? *EH-tuh s^yihr^y-YOHZ-nuh?*

1751. I sleep poorly.
Я пло́хо сплю. *yah PLOH-khuh spl^yoo.*

1752. I have no appetite.
У меня́ нет аппети́та.
oo-m^yih-N^yAH n^yeht ah-p^yih-T^yEE-tuh.

1753. Give me something to relieve the pain.
Да́йте мне что́-нибудь от бо́ли.
DAH_EE-t^yih mn^yeh SHTOH-n^yee-boot^y ahd-BOH-l^yee.

1754. I am allergic to [penicillin].
У меня́ аллерги́я к [пеницилли́ну].
oo-m^yih-N^yAH ah-l^yihr-G^yEE-yuh k[p^yih-n^yee-tsï-L^yEE-noo].

1755. Where can I have this prescription filled?
Где мо́жно доста́ть лека́рство по э́тому реце́пту?
gd^yeh MOHZH-nuh dah-STAHT^y l^yih-KAHR-stvuh pah-EH-tuh-moo r^yih-TSEHP-too?

---

* See footnote on previous page.

1756. Do I have to go [to a hospital] [to an out-patient clinic]?

Мне́ на́до идти́ [в больни́цу] [в поликли́нику]?

mn^yeh NAH-duh eet-T^yEE [vbahl^y-N^yEE-tsoo] [fpuh-l^yee-KL^yEE-n^yee-koo]?

1757. Is surgery required?

Опера́ция необходи́ма?

ah-p^yih-RAH-tsï-yuh n^yih-ahp-khah-D^yEE-muh?

1758. Do I have to stay in bed?

Мне́ на́до лежа́ть в посте́ли?

mn^yeh NAH-duh l^yih-ZHAHT^y fpah-ST^yEH-l^yee?

1759. When will I begin to feel better?

Когда́ я чу́вствую себя́ лу́чше?

kahg-DAH yah CHOOST-voo-yoo s^yih-B^yAH LOOCH-shï?

1760. Is it contagious?

Эта боле́знь зара́зная?

EH-tuh bah-L^yEH-z^yihn^y zah-RAHZ-nuh-yuh?

1761. I feel [better].

Я чу́вствую себя́ [лу́чше].

yah CHOOST-voo-yoo s^yih-B^yAH [LOOCH-shï].

1762. —worse. —ху́же. —*KHOO-zhï.*

1763. —about the same. —та́к же. —*TAHG-zhuh.*

1764. Shall I keep it bandaged?

Повя́зку оста́вить?

pah-V^yAHS-koo ah-STAH-v^yeet^y?

1765. Can I travel [on Monday]?

Мо́жно мне́ путеше́ствовать [в понеде́льник]?

MOHZH-nuh mn^yeh poo-t^yih-SHEHST-vuh-vuht^y [fpuh-n^yih-D^yEHL^y-n^yeek]?

1766. When will you come again?
Когда́ вы́ ещё ра́з придёте?
kahg-DAH vï yih-SHHOH rahs pr^yee-D^yOH-t^yih?

1767. When should I take [the medicine]?
Когда́ мне́ принима́ть [лека́рство]?
kahg-DAH mn^yeh pr^yee-n^yee-MAHT^y
[l^yih-KAHR-stvuh]?

1768. —the pills.
—табле́тки. —*tah-BL^yEHT-k^yee.*

1769. When should I have the injections (immunizing/
curative)?
Когда́ мне́ де́лать приви́вки/уко́лы?
kahg-DAH mn^yeh D^yEH-luht^y pr^yee-V^yEEF-
k^yee/oo-KOH-lï?

1770. Every hour.
Ка́ждый ча́с. *KAHZH-dï_ee chahs.*

1771. [Before] [after] meals.
[До] [по́сле] еды́. *[duh] [POHS-l^yih] yih-Dḯ.*

1772. On going to bed.
Пе́ред сно́м. *P^yEH-r^yiht snohm.*

1773. On getting up. По́сле сна́. *POHS-l^yih snah.*

1774. Twice a day.
Два́ ра́за в де́нь. *dvah RAH-zuh vd^yehn^y.*

1775. An anesthetic.
Анестези́рующее сре́дство.
ah-n^yih-st^yih-Z^yEE-roo-yoo-shhuh-yuh SR^yEHT-stvuh.

1776. Convalescence.
Выздоровле́ние. *vï-zduh-rahv-L^yEH-n^yee-yuh.*

1777. Diet. Дие́та. *d^yee-EH-tuh.*

1778. A drop. Ка́пля. *KAH-pl^yuh.*

1779. A nurse. Медсестра́. *m*ʸ*iht-s*ʸ*ih-STRAH.*

1780. An ophthalmologist.
Окули́ст. *ah-koo-L*ʸ*EEST.*

1781. An orthopedist. Ортопе́д. *ahr-tah-P*ʸ*EHT.*

1782. Remedy.
Лече́бное сре́дство.
*l*ʸ*ih-CHEHB-nuh-yuh SR*ʸ*EHT-stvuh.*

1783. A specialist.
Специали́ст. *sp*ʸ*ih-tsï-ah-L*ʸ*EEST.*

1784. A surgeon. Хиру́рг. *kh*ʸ*ee-ROORK.*

1785. Treatment (OR: **Cure**).
Лече́ние. *l*ʸ*ih-CHEH-n*ʸ*ee-yuh.*

1786. X-ray. Рентге́н. *r*ʸ*ihnd-G*ʸ*EHN.*

AILMENTS

1787. An abscess. Нары́в. *nah-RÏF.*

1788. An allergy. Аллерги́я. *ah-l*ʸ*ihr-G*ʸ*EE-yuh.*

1789. An appendicitis attack.
При́ступ аппендици́та.
*PR*ʸ*EE-stoop ah-p*ʸ*ihn-d*ʸ*ee-TSÏ-tuh.*

1790. Asthma. А́стма. *AHST-muh.*

1791. An insect bite.
Уку́с насеко́мого. *oo-KOOS nuh-s*ʸ*ih-KOH-muh-vuh.*

1792. A blister. Волды́рь. *vahl-DÏR*ʸ*.*

1793. A boil. Фуру́нкл. *foo-ROON-kuhl.*

1794. A bruise. Синя́к. *s*ʸ*ee-N*ʸ*AHK.*

1795. A burn. Ожёг. *ah-ZHOHK.*

1796. Chicken pox. Ветря́нка. *v*ʸ*ih-TR*ʸ*AHN-kuh.*

1797. A chill. Озноб. *ahz-NOHP.*

1798. A cold.
Простуда (OR: Насморк).
prah-STOO-duh (OR: *NAH-smuhrk*).

1799. Constipation. Запор. *zah-POHR.*

1800. A corn. Мозоль. *mah-ZOHL^y.*

1801. A cough. Кашель. *KAH-shïl^y.*

1802. A cramp. Судорога. *SOO-duh-ruh-guh.*

1803. A cut. Порез. *pah-R^yEHS.*

1804. Diarrhea. Понос. *pah-NOHS.*

1805. Dysentery.
Дизентерия. *d^yee-z^yihn-t^yih-R^yEE-yuh.*

1806. An earache. Боль в ухе. *bohl^y VOO-kh^yih.*

1807. An epidemic.
Эпидемия. *eh-p^yee-D^yEH-m^yee-yuh.*

1808. To feel faint.
Чувствовать дурноту.
CHOOST-vuh-vuht^y door-nah-TOO.

1809. A fever. Лихорадка. *l^yee-khah-RAHT-kuh.*

1810. A fracture. Перелом. *p^yih-r^yih-LOHM.*

1811. Hay fever.
Сенная лихорадка.
s^yihn-NAH-yuh l^yee-khah-RAHT-kuh.

1812. Headache.
Головная боль. *guh-lahv-NAH-yuh bohl^y.*

1813. High blood pressure.
Гипертония. *g^yee-p^yihr-tah-N^yEE-yuh.*

1814. Indigestion.
Несварение желудка.
n^yih-svah-R^yEH-n^yee-yuh zhï-LOOT-kuh.

1815. Infection.
Инфе́кция. *een-F ʸEHK-tsï-yuh.*

1816. Inflammation.
Воспале́ние. *vuh-spah-L ʸEH-n ʸee-yuh.*

1817. Influenza. Гри́пп. *gr ʸeep.*

1818. Insomnia.
Бессо́нница. *b ʸis-SOHN-n ʸee-tsuh.*

1819. Measles. Ко́рь. *kohr ʸ.*

1820. German measles.
Красну́ха. *krahs-NOO-khuh.*

1821. Mumps. Сви́нка. *SV ʸEEN-kuh.*

1822. Nausea. Тошнота́. *tuhsh-nah-TAH.*

1823. Nosebleed.
Носово́е кровотече́ние.
nuh-sah-VOH-yuh kruh-vuh-t ʸih-CHEH-n ʸee-yuh.

1824. Pneumonia.
Воспале́ние лёгких (OR: Пневноми́я).
vuhs-pah-L ʸEH-n ʸee-yuh L ʸOHKH-k ʸeekh (OR:
pn ʸihv-nah-M ʸEE-yuh).

1825. Poisoning.
Отравле́ние. *ah-trahv-L ʸEH-n ʸee-yuh.*

1826. A sore throat. Ангина́. *ahn-G ʸEE-nuh.*

1827. A sprain. Вы́вих. *VÏ-v ʸeekh.*

1828. A bee sting. Уку́с пчелы́. *oo-KOOS pchih-LÏ.*

1829. A sunburn.
Со́лнечный ожо́г. *SOHL-n ʸihch-nï_ee ah-ZHOHK.*

1830. A swelling. О́пухоль. *OH-poo-khuhl ʸ.*

1831. Tonsillitis. Тонзилли́т. *tuhn-z ʸee-L ʸEET.*

1832. Stomach ulcer.
Я́зва желу́дка. *YAHZ-vuh zhï-LOOT-kuh.*

1833. To vomit. Рвать. *rvaht^y.*

See also "Accidents," p. 155, "Parts of the Body," p. 157, and "Pharmacy," p. 121.

DENTIST

1834. Can you recommend [a good dentist]?
Порекомендуйте [хорошего зубного врача].
puh-r^yih-kuh-m^yihn-DOO‿EE-t^yih [khah-ROH-shuh-vuh zoob-NOH-vuh vrah-CHAH].

1835. I have lost a filling (LIT.: **My filling fell out**).
У меня выпала пломба.
oo-m^yih-N^yAH VĬ-puh-luh PLOHM-buh.

1836. Can you replace [the filling]?
Вы можете поставить новую [пломбу]?
vï MOH-zhuh-t^yih pah-STAH-v^yeet^y NOH-voo-yoo [PLOHM-boo]?

1837. Can you fix [the bridge]?
Вы можете починить [мост]?
vï MOH-zhuh-t^yih puh-chee-N^yEET^y [mohst]?

1838. —this denture.
—этот зубной протез.
—EH-tuht zoob-NOY prah-T^yEHS.

1839. This [tooth] hurts me.
Этот [зуб] болит. *EH-tuht [zoop] bah-L^yEET.*

1840. My gums are sore.
У меня дёсны болят.
oo-m^yih-N^yAH D^yOHS-nï bah-L^yAHT.

1841. I have [a broken tooth] [a toothache].
У меня [сломался зуб] [зубная боль].
oo-m^{y}ih-N^{y}AH [slah-MAHL-suh zoop]
  [zoob-NAH-yuh bohl^y].

1842. —a cavity. —дупло. *—doo-PLOH.*

1843. Please give me [a general anesthetic].
Прошу [общий наркоз].
prah-SHOO [OHP-shhee nahr-KOHS].

1844. —a local anesthetic.
—местный наркоз. *—M^{y}EHS-nï_ee nahr-KOHS.*

1845. I [do not] want the tooth extracted.
Я [не] хочу, чтобы вы вырвали зуб.
yah [n^{y}ih]-khah-CHOO, SHTOH-bï vï VÏR-vuh-l^{y}ee
  zoop.

1846. A temporary filling.
Временная пломба.
VR^{y}EH-m^{y}ihn-nuh-yuh PLOHM-buh.

ACCIDENTS

1847. There has been an accident.
Произошёл несчастный случай.
pruh-ee-zah-SHOHL n^{y}ih-SHHAHS-nï_ee
  SLOO-chih_ee.

1848. Get [a doctor] immediately.
Позовите [доктора] сейчас же.
puh-zah-V^{y}EE-t^{y}ih [DOHK-tuh-ruh]
  s^{y}ih-CHAHZH-zhuh.

1849. —a policeman. —милиционера. *—m^{y}ee-l^{y}ee-tsï-ah-N^{y}EH-ruh.*

1850. Get an ambulance immediately.
Вы́зовите "ско́рую по́мощь" сейча́с же.
VĬ-zuh-vʸee-tʸih " SKOH-roo-yoo POH-mushh"
sʸih-CHAHZH-zhuh.

1851. He has fallen. Он упа́л. *ohn oo-PAHL.*

1852. She has fallen.
Она́ упа́ла. *ah-NAH oo-PAH-luh.*

1853. [He] [she] has fainted.
[Он упа́л] [она́ упа́ла] в о́бморок.
[ohn oo-PAHL] [ah-NAH oo-PAH-luh] VOHB-muh-ruhk.

1854. Do not move [him] [her].
Не дви́гайте [его́] [её].
nʸih-DVʸEE-guh_ee-tʸih [yih-VOH] [yih-YOH].

1855. [My finger] is bleeding.
[Мой па́лец] кровото́чит.
[moy PAH-lʸihts] kruh-vah-TOH-chiht.

1856. A fracture [of the arm].
Перело́м [руки́]. *pʸih-rʸih-LOHM [roo-KʸEE].*

1857. I want [to rest] [to sit down] [to lie down].
Я хочу́ [отдохну́ть] [сесть] [лечь].
yah khah-CHOO [ahd-dahkh-NOOTʸ] [sʸehstʸ]
[lʸehch].

1858. Notify [my husband] [my wife].
Сообщи́те [моему́ му́жу] [мое́й жене́].
sah-ahp-SHHEE-tʸih [muh-yih-MOO MOO-zhoo]
[mah-YEH_EE zhï-NʸEH].

1859. A tourniquet. Турнике́т. *toor-nʸee-KʸEHT.*

PARTS OF THE BODY

1860. Ankle. Лодыжка. *lah-DÏSH-kuh.*

1861. Appendix. Аппе́ндикс. *ah-P^{y}EHN-d^{y}eeks.*

1862. Arm. Рука́. *roo-KAH.*

1863. Armpit. Подмы́шка. *pahd-MÏSH-kuh.*

1864. Artery. Арте́рия. *ahr-T^{y}EH-r^{y}ee-yuh.*

1865. Back. Спина́. *sp^{y}ee-NAH.*

1866. Belly. Живо́т. *zhï-VOHT.*

1867. Blood. Кро́вь. *krohf^y.*

1868. Blood vessel.
Кровено́сный сосу́д.
kruh-v^{y}ih-NOHS-nï͟ee sah-SOOT.

1869. Body. Те́ло. *T^{y}EH-luh.*

1870. Bone. Ко́сть. *kohst^y.*

1871. Bowel. Кише́чник. *k^{y}ee-SHEHCH-n^{y}eek.*

1872. Brain. Мо́зг. *mohsk.*

1873. Breasts. Гру́ди. *GROO-d^{y}ee.*

1874. Calf. Икра́. *ee-KRAH.*

1875. Cheek. Щека́. *shhih-KAH.*

1876. Chest (OR: **Breast**). Грудь. *groot^y.*

1877. Chin. Подборо́док. *puhd-bah-ROH-duhk.*

1878. Collarbone. Ключи́ца. *kl^{y}oo-CHEE-tsuh.*

1879. Ear. У́хо. *OO-khuh.*

1880. Elbow. Ло́коть. *LOH-kuht^y.*

1881. Eye. Гла́з. *glahs.*

1882. Eyelashes. Ресни́цы. *r^{y}ihs-N^{y}EE-tsï.*

1883. Eyelid. Ве́ко. *V^{y}EH-kuh.*

1884. Face. Лицо́. *l^yee-TSOH*.

1885. Finger. Па́лец. *PAH-l^yihts*.

1886. Fingernail. Но́готь. *NOH-guht^y*.

1887. Foot.
Нога́ (OR: Ступня́).* *nah-GAH* (OR: *stoop-N^yAH*).

1888. Forehead. Лоб. *lohp*.

1889. Gall bladder.
Жёлчный пузы́рь. *ZHOHLCH-nï‿ee poo-ZÏR^y*.

1890. Genitals.
Половы́е о́рганы. *puh-lah-VÏ-yih OHR-guh-nï*.

1891. Glands. Же́лезы. *ZHEH-l^yih-zï*.

1892. Hand.
Рука́ (OR: Кисть).† *roo-KAH* (OR: *k^yeest^y*).

1893. Head. Голова́. *guh-lah-VAH*.

1894. Heart. Се́рдце. *S^yEHR-tsuh*.

1895. Heel. Пя́тка. *P^yAHT-kuh*.

1896. Hip.
Бедро́ (leg from knee to waist). *b^yih-DROH*.

1897. Intestines. Кишки́. *k^yeesh-K^yEE*.

1898. Jaw. Че́люсть. *CHEH-l^yoost^y*.

1899. Joint. Суста́в. *soo-STAHF*.

1900. Kidney. По́чка. *POHCH-kuh*.

---

* The word нога́ (*nah-GAH*) is normally used for both foot and leg in Russian. Ступня́ (*stoop-N^yAH*) is used when speaking of the foot as opposed to the leg.

† The word рука́ (*roo-KAH*) is normally used for both hand and arm in Russian. Кисть (*k^yeest^y*) is used when speaking of the hand as opposed to the arm.

1901. Knee. Коле́но. *kah-L^{y}EH-nuh.*

1902. Larynx. Горта́нь. *gahr-TAHN^y.*

1903. Leg. Нога́. *nah-GAH.*

1904. Lip. Губа́. *goo-BAH.*

1905. Liver. Пе́чень. *P^{y}EH-chihn^y.*

1906. Lungs. Лёгкие. *L^{y}OHKH-k^{y}ee-yih.*

1907. Mouth. Рот. *roht.*

1908. Muscle. Мы́шца. *MЇSH-tsuh.*

1909. Navel. Пупо́к. *poo-POHK.*

1910. Neck. Ше́я. *SHEH-yuh.*

1911. Nerve. Нерв. *n^{y}ehrf.*

1912. Nose. Нос. *nohs.*

1913. Pancreas.
Поджелу́дочная железа́.
puhd-zhЇ-LOO-duhch-nuh-yuh zhЇ-l^{y}ih-ZAH.

1914. Rib. Ребро́. *r^{y}ih-BROH.*

1915. Shoulder. Плечо́. *pl^{y}ih-CHOH.*

1916. Side. Бок. *bohk.*

1917. Skin. Ко́жа. *KOH-zhuh.*

1918. Skull. Че́реп. *CHEH-r^{y}ihp.*

1919. Spine.
Позвоно́чник. *puhz-vah-NOHCH-n^{y}eek.*

1920. Spleen.
Селезёнка. *s^{y}ih-l^{y}ih-Z^{y}OHN-kuh.*

1921. Stomach. Желу́док. *zhЇ-LOO-duhk.*

1922. Temple. Висо́к. *v^{y}ee-SOHK.*

1923. Thigh. Бедро́. *b^{y}ih-DROH.*

1924. Throat. Го́рло. *GOHR-luh.*

1925. Thumb.
Большо́й па́лец. *bahl^y-SHOY PAH-l^yihts.*

1926. Toe. Па́лец (ноги́). *PAH-l^yihts (nah-G^yEE).*

1927. Tongue. Язы́к. *yih-ZŸK.*

1928. Tonsils.
Гла́нды (OR: Минда́лины).
GLAHN-dï (OR: m^yeen-DAH-l^yee-nï).

1929. Vein. Ве́на. *V^yEH-nuh.*

1930. Waist. Та́лия. *TAH-l^yee-yuh.*

1931. Wrist. Запя́стье. *zah-P^yAHST^y-yuh.*

TIME*

1932. What time is it?
Кото́рый ча́с? *kah-TOH-rï⌣ee chahs?*

1933. One o'clock [A.M.] [P.M.].
Ча́с [но́чи] [дня́]. *chahs [NOH-chee] [dn^yah].*

1934. Two [A.M.] [P.M.].
Два́ часа́ [но́чи] [дня́].
dvah chih-SAH [NOH-chee] [dn^yah].

1935. Seven [A.M.] [P.M.].
Се́мь часо́в [утра́] [ве́чера].
s^yehm^y chih-SOHF [oo-TRAH] [V^yEH-chih-ruh].

---

* Official time (radio, television, newspapers, public notices) in the Soviet Union is given according to a 24-hour clock, e.g. 1:00 P.M. = 13:00. Official time also employs a straightforward counting system, e.g. 5:45, "five-forty-five" = пя́ть со́рок пя́ть (*p^yaht^y SOH-ruhk p^yaht^y*).

1936. It is exactly half-past three (LIT.: Exactly half of the fourth, that is, a half into the fourth hour).

Ро́вно полови́на четвёртого.

ROHV-nuh puh-lah-V^yEE-nuh chiht–V^yOHR-tuh-vuh.

1937. Quarter-past four (LIT.: A quarter of the fifth).

Че́тверть пя́того.   *CHEHT-v^yihrt^y P^yAH-tuh-vuh.*

1938. Quarter to five (LIT.: Five less a quarter).

Без че́тверти пять.   *b^yihs-CHEHT-v^yihr-t^yee p^yaht^y.*

1939. At ten (minutes) to six (LIT.: Six less ten minutes).

Без десяти́ (мину́т) шесть.

b^yihz-d^yih-s^yih-T^yEE (m^yee-NOOT) shehst^y.

1940. At twenty (minutes) past seven (LIT.: Twenty minutes of the eighth).

В два́дцать (мину́т) восьмо́го.

VDVAHT-tsuht^y (m^yee-NOOT) vahs^y-MOH-vuh.

1941. It is early.   Ра́но.   *RAH-nuh.*

1942. [He] [She] is late.

[Он] [Она́] опа́здывает.

[ohn] [ah-NAH] ah-PAH-zdï-vuh-yiht.

1943. In the morning.   У́тром.   *OO-truhm.*

1944. This afternoon.

Сего́дня днём (OR: По́сле обе́да).

s^yih-VOHD-n^yuh dn^yohm (OR: POHS-l^yih ah-B^yEH-duh).

1945. Tomorrow.   За́втра.   *ZAHF-truh.*

1946. In the evening.

Ве́чером.   *V^yEH-chih-ruhm.*

1947. At noon.   В по́лдень.   *FPOHL-d^yihn^y.*

1948. At midnight.   В по́лночь.   *FPOHL-nuhch.*

1949. During the day.

В тече́ние дня.   *ft^yih-CHEH-n^yee-yuh dn^yah.*

1950. Every evening.
Ка́ждый ве́чер. *KAHZH-dï_ee V^yEH-chihr.*

1951. Every night.
Ка́ждую но́чь. *KAHZH-doo-yoo nohch.*

1952. All night. Всю но́чь. *fs^yoo nohch.*

1953. Yesterday. Вчера́. *vchih-RAH.*

1954. Today. Сего́дня. *s^yih-VOHD-n^yuh.*

1955. Tonight.
Сего́дня ве́чером. *s^yih-VOHD-n^yuh V^yEH-chih-ruhm.*

1956. Last month.
В про́шлом ме́сяце.
FPROHSH-luhm M^yEH-s^yih-tsï.

1957. Last year.
В про́шлом году́. *FPROHSH-luhm gah-DOO.*

1958. Next Sunday.
В бу́дущее воскресе́нье.
VBOO-doo-shhuh-yuh vuhs-kr^yih-S^yEHN^y-yuh.

1959. Next week.
На бу́дущей неде́ле.
nah-BOO-doo-shhih_ee n^yih-D^yEH-l^yih.

1960. The day before yesterday.
Позавчера́. *puh-zuhf-chih-RAH.*

1961. The day after tomorrow.
По́слеза́втра. *POHS-l^yih-ZAHF-truh.*

1962. Two weeks ago.
Две́ неде́ли наза́д. *dv^yeh n^yih-D^yEH-l^yee nah-ZAHT.*

WEATHER

1963. How is the weather today?
Какая сегодня погода?
kah-KAH-yuh s^yih-VOHD-n^yuh pah-GOH-duh?

1964. It looks like rain.
Похоже, что будет дождь.
pah-KHOH-zhï-shtut BOO-d^yiht dohsht^y.

1965. It is raining.   Идёт дождь.   *ee-D^YOHT dohsht^y.*

1966. It is [cold].
Сейчас [холодно].   *s^yih-CHAHS [KHOH-luhd-nuh].*

1967. —fair.
—хорошая погода.
—khah-ROH-shuh-yuh pah-GOH-duh.

1968. —warm.   —тепло.   *—t^yih-PLOH.*

1969. —windy.   —ветренно.   *—V^yEH-tr^yihn-nuh.*

1970. The weather is clearing.
(Погода) проясняется.
(pah-GOH-duh) pruh-yihs-N^yAH-yiht-tsuh.

1971. What a beautiful day!
Какой прекрасный день!
kah-KOY pr^yih-KRAHS-nï_ee d^yehn^y!

1972. I want to sit [in the shade].
Я хочу сидеть [в тени].
yah khah-CHOO s^yee-D^YEHT^y [ft^yih-N^YEE].

1973. —in the sun.   —на солнце.   *—nah-SOHN-tsï.*

1974. —in the breeze.
—на ветерке.   *—nuh-v^yih-t^yihr-K^yEH.*

1975. What is the weather forecast [for tomorrow]?
Какой прогноз погоды [на завтра]?
kah-KOY prahg-NOHS pah-GOH-dï [nah-ZAHF-truh]?

1976. —for the weekend.
—на суббо́ту и воскресе́нье.
—*nuh-soo-BOH-too ee vuhs-kr^yih-S^yEHN^y-yuh.*

1977. It will snow tomorrow.
За́втра бу́дет снег. *ZAHF-truh BOO-d^yiht sn^yehk.*

DAYS OF THE WEEK

1978. Sunday. Воскресе́нье. *vuhs-kr^yih-S^yEHN^y-yuh.*

1979. Monday.
Понеде́льник. *puh-n^yih-D^yEHL^y-n^yeek.*

1980. Tuesday. Вто́рник. *FTOHR-n^yeek.*

1981. Wednesday. Среда́. *sr^yih-DAH.*

1982. Thursday. Четве́рг. *chiht-V^yEHRK.*

1983. Friday. Пя́тница. *P^yAHT-n^yee-tsuh.*

1984. Saturday. Суббо́та. *soo-BOH-tuh.*

HOLIDAYS

1985. A public holiday. Пра́здник. *PRAHZ-n^yeek.*

1986. Happy Hanukkah.
С Ха́нукой. *SKHAH-noo-kuh＿ee.*

1987. Christmas.
Рождество́ Христо́во.
ruhzh-d^yih-STVOH khr^yee-STOH-vuh.

1988. Merry Christmas.
С Рождество́м Христо́вым.
sruhzh-d^yih-STVOHM khr^yee-STOH-vïm.

1989. Happy Easter (OR: **Happy Passover**).
С Па́схой. *SPAHS-khuh＿ee.*

1990. Happy New Year.
С Но́вым го́дом.   *SNOH-vïm GOH-duhm.*

1991. Happy birthday.
С днём рожде́ния.   *zdnʸohm rahzh-DʸEH-nʸee-yuh.*

1992. Happy anniversary.
С годовщи́ной.   *zguh-dahf-SHHEE-nuh⌣ee.*

1993. A religious holiday.
Религио́зный пра́здник.
rʸih-lʸee-gʸee-OHZ-nï⌣ee PRAHZ-nʸeek.

DATES, MONTHS AND SEASONS

1994. January.   Янва́рь.   *yihn-VAHRʸ.*

1995. February.   Февра́ль.   *fʸih-VRAHLʸ.*

1996. March.   Март.   *mahrt.*

1997. April.   Апре́ль.   *ah-PRʸEHLʸ.*

1998. May.   Май.   *mah⌣ee.*

1999. June.   Ию́нь.   *ee-YOONʸ.*

2000. July.   Ию́ль.   *ee-YOOLʸ.*

2001. August.   А́вгуст.   *AHV-goost.*

2002. September.   Сентя́брь.   *sʸihn-TʸAH-buhrʸ.*

2003. October.   Октя́брь.   *ahk-TʸAH-buhrʸ.*

2004. November.   Ноя́брь.   *nah-YAH-buhrʸ.*

2005. December.   Декабрь.   *dʸih-KAH-buhrʸ.*

2006. The spring.   Весна́.   *vʸihs-NAH.*

2007. The summer.   Ле́то.   *LʸEH-tuh.*

2008. The autumn.   О́сень.   *OH-sʸihnʸ.*

2009. The winter.   Зима́.   *zʸee-MAH.*

NUMBERS: CARDINALS

2010. Zero. Ну́ль (OR: Но́ль). *nool^y* (OR: *nohl^y*).

2011. One.
Оди́н (F.: одна́) (N.: одно́).
ah-D^{y}EEN (F.: *ahd-NAH*) (N.: *ahd-NOH*).

2012. Two. Два́ (F.: две́). *dvah* (F.: *dv^{y}eh*).

2013. Three. Три́. *tr^{y}ee.*

2014. Four. Четы́ре. *chih-TЇ-r^{y}ih.*

2015. Five. Пя́ть. *p^{y}aht^y.*

2016. Six. Ше́сть. *shehst^y.*

2017. Seven. Се́мь. *s^{y}ehm^y.*

2018. Eight. Во́семь. *VOH-s^{y}ihm^y.*

2019. Nine. Де́вять. *D^{y}EH-v^{y}iht^y.*

2020. Ten. Де́сять. *D^{y}EH-s^{y}iht^y.*

2021. Eleven. Оди́ннадцать. *ah-D^{y}EEN-nuht-tsuht^y.*

2022. Twelve. Двена́дцать. *dv^{y}ih-NAHT-tsuht^y.*

2023. Thirteen. Трина́дцать. *tr^{y}ee-NAHT-tsuht^y.*

2024. Fourteen.
Четы́рнадцать. *chih-TЇR-nuht-tsuht^y.*

2025. Fifteen. Пятна́дцать. *p^{y}iht-NAHT-tsuht^y.*

2026. Sixteen. Шестна́дцать. *shïs-NAHT-tsuht^y.*

2027. Seventeen. Семна́дцать. *s^{y}ihm-NAHT-tsuht^y.*

2028. Eighteen.
Восемна́дцать. *vuh-s^{y}ihm-NAHT-tsuht^y.*

2029. Nineteen.
Девятна́дцать. *d^{y}ih-v^{y}iht-NAHT-tsuht^y.*

2030. Twenty. Два́дцать. *DVAHT-tsuht*^{y}.

2031. Twenty-one.
Два́дцать оди́н (F.: одна́) (N.: одно́).
DVAHT-tsuht^y *ah-D*^{y}*EEN* (F.: *ahd-NAH*)
(N.: *ahd-NOH*).

2032. Twenty-five.
Два́дцать пять. *DVAHT-tsuht*^{y} *p*^{y}*aht*^{y}.

2033. Thirty. Три́дцать. *TR*^{y}*EET-tsuht*^{y}.

2034. Forty. Со́рок. *SOH-ruhk*.

2035. Fifty. Пятьдеся́т. *p*^{y}*ihd*^{y}*-d*^{y}*ih-S*^{y}*AHT*.

2036. Sixty. Шестьдеся́т. *shïz*^{y}*-d*^{y}*ih-S*^{y}*AHT*.

2037. Seventy. Се́мьдесят. *S*^{y}*EHM*^{y}*-d*^{y}*ih-s*^{y}*iht*.

2038. Eighty.
Во́семьдесят. *VOH-s*^{y}*ihm*^{y}*-d*^{y}*ih-s*^{y}*iht*.

2039. Ninety.
Девяно́ста. *d*^{y}*ih-v*^{y}*ih-NOH-stuh*.

2040. One hundred. Сто́. *stoh*.

2041. One hundred one.
Сто́ оди́н (F.: одна́) (N.: одно́).
stoh ah-D^y*EEN* (F.: *ahd-NAH*) (N.: *ahd-NOH*).

2042. One hundred ten.
Сто́ де́сять. *stoh D*^{y}*EH-s*^{y}*iht*^{y}.

2043. One thousand.
Ты́сяча. *TÏ-s*^{y}*ih-chuh*.

2044. Two thousand.
Две́ ты́сячи. *dv*^{y}*eh TÏ-s*^{y}*ih-chee*.

2045. Three thousand.
Три́ ты́сячи. *tr*^{y}*ee TÏ-s*^{y}*ih-chee*.

2046. Five thousand. Пять ты́сяч. *p*^{y}*aht*^{y} *TÏ-s*^{y}*ihch*.

2047. One hundred thousand.
Сто́ ты́сяч. *stoh TЇ-s*ʸ*ihch.*

2048. One million. Миллио́н. *m*ʸ*ee-l*ʸ*ee-OHN.*

NUMBERS: ORDINALS

2049. The first.
Пе́рвый (F.: пе́рвая) (N.: пе́рвое).
*P*ʸ*EHR-vï‿ee* (F.: *P*ʸ*EHR-vuh-yuh*)
  (N.: *P*ʸ*EHR-vuh-yuh*).

2050. The second.
Второ́й (F.: втора́я) (N.: второ́е).
ftah-ROY (F.: *ftah-RAH-yuh*) (N.: *ftah-ROH-yuh*).

2051. The third.
Тре́тий (F.: тре́тья) (N.: тре́тье).
*TR*ʸ*EH-t*ʸ*ee* (F.: *TR*ʸ*EHT*ʸ*-yuh*) (N.: *TR*ʸ*EHT*ʸ*-yuh*).

2052. The fourth.
Четвёртый (F.: четвёртая) (N.: четвёртое).
*chiht-V*ʸ*OHR-tï‿ee* (F.: *chiht-V*ʸ*OHR-tuh-yuh*)
  (N.: *chiht-V*ʸ*OHR-tuh-yuh*).

2053. The fifth.
Пя́тый (F.: пя́тая) (N.: пя́тое).
*P*ʸ*AH-tï‿ee* (F.: *P*ʸ*AH-tuh-yuh*) (N.: *P*ʸ*AH-tuh-yuh*).

2054. The sixth.
Шесто́й (F.: шеста́я) (N.: шесто́е).
shï-STOY (F.: *shï-STAH-yuh*) (N.: *shï-STOH-yuh*).

2055. The seventh.
Седьмо́й (F.: седьма́я) (N.: седьмо́е).
*s*ʸ*ihd*ʸ*-MOY* (F.: *s*ʸ*ihd*ʸ*-MAH-yuh*)
  (N.: *s*ʸ*ihd*ʸ*-MOH-yuh*).

2056. The eighth.
Восьмо́й (F.: восьма́я) (N.: восьмо́е).
vahs^y-MOY (F.: *vahs^y-MAH-yuh*) (N.: *vahs^y-MOH-yuh*).

2057. The ninth.
Девя́тый (F.: девя́тая) (N.: девя́тое).
d^yih-V^yAH-tï_ee (F.: *d^yih-V^yAH-tuh-yuh*)
   (N.: *d^yih-V^yAH-tuh-yuh*).

2058. The tenth.
Деся́тый (F.: деся́тая) (N.: деся́тое).
d^yih-S^yAH-tï_ee (F.: *d^yih-S^yAH-tuh-yuh*)
   (N.: *d^yih-S^yAH-tuh-yuh*).

2059. The twentieth.
Двадца́тый (F.: двадца́тая) (N.: двадца́тое).
dvaht-TSAH-tï_ee (F.: *dvaht-TSAH-tuh-yuh*)
   (N.: *dvaht-TSAH-tuh-yuh*).

2060. The thirtieth.
Тридца́тый (F.: тридца́тая) (N.: тридца́тое).
tr^yeet-TSAH-tï_ee (F.: *tr^yeet-TSAH-tuh-yuh*)
   (N.: *tr^yeet-TSAH-tuh-yuh*).

2061. The hundredth.
Со́тый (F.: со́тая) (N.: со́тое).
SOH-tï_ee (F.: *SOH-tuh-yuh*) (N.: *SOH-tuh-yuh*).

2062. The thousandth.
Ты́сячный (F.: ты́сячная) (N.: ты́сячное).
TÏ-s^yihch-nï_ee (F.: *TÏ-s^yihch-nuh-yuh*)
   (N.: *TÏ-s^yihch-nuh-yuh*).

2063. The millionth.
Миллио́нный (F.: миллио́нная) (N.: миллио́нное).
m^yee-l^yee-OHN-nï_ee (F.: *m^yee-l^yee-OHN-nuh-yuh*)
   (N.: *m^yee-l^yee-OHN-nuh-yuh*).

QUANTITIES

2064. A fraction. Дробь. *drohp^y*.

2065. One-quarter.
Одна четверть. *ahd-NAH CHEHT-v^{y}ihrt^y*.

2066. One-third.
Одна треть. *ahd-NAH tr^{y}eht^y*.

2067. One-half.
(Одна) половина. *(ahd-NAH) puh-lah-V^{y}EE-nuh*.

2068. Three-quarters.
Три четверти. *tr^{y}ee CHEHT-v^{y}ihr-t^{y}ee*.

2069. The whole. Целое. *TSEH-luh-yuh*.

2070. A little (OR: **A few**). Немного. *n^{y}ihm-NOH-guh*.

2071. Several. Несколько. *N^{y}EH-skuhl^y-kuh*.

2072. Many (OR: **Much**). Много. *MNOH-guh*.

FAMILY

2073. Wife (OR: **Spouse**).
Жена (OR: Супруга). *zhï-NAH* (OR: *soo-PROO-guh*).

2074. Husband (OR: **Spouse**).
Муж (OR: Супруг). *moosh* (OR: *soo-PROOK*).

2075. Mother. Мать. *maht^y*.

2076. Father. Отец. *ah-T^{y}EHTS*.

2077. Grandmother. Бабушка. *BAH-boosh-kuh*.

2078. Grandfather. Дедушка. *D^{y}EH-doosh-kuh*.

2079. Daughter. Дочь. *dohch*.

2080. Son. Сын. *sïn*.

2081. Sister. Сестра́. *s^{y}ih-STRAH.*

2082. Brother. Бра́т. *braht.*

2083. Aunt. Тётя. *T^{y}OH-t^{y}uh.*

2084. Uncle. Дя́дя. *D^{y}AH-d^{y}uh.*

2085. Niece. Племя́нница. *pl^{y}ih-M^{y}AHN-n^{y}ee-tsuh.*

2086. Nephew. Племя́нник. *pl^{y}ih-M^{y}AHN-n^{y}eek.*

2087. Cousin.
Двою́родный бра́т (F.: Двою́родная сестра́).
dvah-YOO-ruhd-nï̆_ee braht (F.: dvah-YOO-ruhd-nuh-yuh s^{y}ih-STRAH).

2088. Relative. Ро́дственник. *ROHT-stv^{y}ihn-n^{y}eek.*

2089. Father-in-law (husband's father/wife's father).
Свёкор/Те́сть. *SV^{y}OH-kuhr/t^{y}ehst^y.*

2090. Mother-in-law (husband's mother/wife's mother).
Свекро́вь/Тёща. *sv^{y}ih-KROHF^y/T^{y}OH-shhuh.*

2091. Adults. Взро́слые. *VZROHS-lï̆-yih.*

2092. Children. Де́ти. *D^{y}EH-t^{y}ee.*

COMMON SIGNS AND
PUBLIC NOTICES

Alphabetized according to the Russian.

2093. [Без де́ла] не входи́ть.
[b^{y}ihz-D^{y}EH-luh] n^{y}ih-fkhah-D^{y}EET^y.
No admittance [except on business].

2094. Береги́сь автомоби́ля!
b^{y}ih-r^{y}ih-G^{y}EES^y ahf-tuh-mah-B^{y}EE-l^{y}uh!
Watch out for cars.

2095. Береги́сь, зла́я соба́ка!
b^{y}ih-r^{y}ih-G^{y}EES^y, ZLAH-yuh sah-BAH-kuh!
Beware of the dog.

2096. Беспла́тно. *b^{y}ihs-PLAHT-nuh.* Free.

2097. Библиоте́ка.
b^{y}ee-bl^{y}ee-ah-T^{y}EH-kuh. Library.

2098. Биле́тная ка́сса.
b^{y}ee-L^{y}EHT-nuh-yuh KAHS-suh.
Ticket office (OR: Box office).

2099. Больни́ца. *bahl^y-N^{y}EE-tsuh.* Hospital.

2100. Буфе́т. *boo-F^{y}EHT.* Buffet.

2101. В ремо́нте.
vr^{y}ih-MOHN-t^{y}ih. Under repair (OR: Men at work).

2102. Ваго́н для куря́щих.
vah-GOHN dl^{y}uh-koo-R^{y}AH-shheekh.
Smoking car.

2103. Ваго́н-рестора́н.
vah-GOHN–r^{y}ih-stah-RAHN.
Dining car (OR: Diner).

2104. Вверх. *vv^{y}ehrkh.* Up.

2105. Вниз. *vn^{y}ees.* Down.

2106. Внима́ние.
vn^{y}ee-MAH-n^{y}ee-yuh. Attention (OR: Warning).

2107. Вокза́л. *vahg-ZAHL.* Railroad station.

2108. Воспреща́ется.
vuhs-pr^{y}ih-SHHAH-yiht-tsuh.
(Is) forbidden (OR: prohibited).

2109. Все́ биле́ты про́даны.
fs^{y}eh b^{y}ee-L^{y}EH-tï PROH-duh-nï. All tickets sold.

2110. Вска́кивать и соска́кивать на ходу́ стро́го воспреща́ется.
FSKAH-k ʸee-vuht ʸ ee sah-SKAH-k ʸee-vuht ʸ nuh-khah-DOO STROH-guh vuhs-pr ʸih-SHHAH-yiht-tsuh.
Jumping on and off while train is in motion is strictly prohibited.

2111. Второй за́втрак.
ftah-ROY ZAHF-truhk. Light lunch.

2112. Вхо́д. *fkhoht.* Entrance (OR: In).

2113. Вхо́д беспла́тный.
vkhohd b ʸihs-PLAHT-ni ̱_ee. Free admission.

2114. Вхо́д в зри́тельный за́л.
fkhoht VZR ʸEE-t ʸihl ʸ-ni ̱_ee zahl.
Entrance to the auditorium.

2115. Вы́годная поку́пка.
VĬ-guhd-nuh-yuh pah-KOOP-kuh. Bargain.

2116. Вы́дача багажа́.
VĬ-duh-chuh buh-gah-ZHAH. Baggage claim.

2117. Вы́ход. *VĬ-khuht.* Exit (OR: Out).

2118. (Вы́ход) в го́род.
(VĬ-khuht) VGOH-ruht.
(Exit) to town (from subway or railroad station).

2119. (Вы́ход) на поса́дку.
(VĬ-khuht) nuh-pah-SAHT-koo. Boarding gate.

2120. Газиро́ванная вода́ [с сиро́пом] [без сиро́па].
guh-z ʸee-ROH-vuhn-nuh-yuh vah-DAH [ss ʸee-ROH-puhm] [b ʸihs-s ʸee-ROH-puh].
[Flavored] [plain] carbonated water.

2121. Гардеро́б.
guhr-d ʸih-ROHP. Checkroom (OR: Cloakroom).

2122. Городско́й сове́т.
guh-raht-SKOY sah-V^{y}EHT.   City hall.

2123. Горя́чая (вода́).
gah-R^{y}AH-chuh-yuh (vah-DAH).   Hot (water).

2124. Держи́тесь [ле́вой] [пра́вой] стороны́.
d^{y}ihr-ZHĬ-t^{y}ihs^y [L^{y}EH-vuh＿ee] [PRAH-vuh＿ee]
stuh-rah-NĬ.
Keep to the [left] [right].

2125. До востре́бования.
duh-vahs-TR^{y}EH-buh-vuh-n^{y}ee-yuh.   General delivery.

2126. До́м в аре́нду.
dohm vah-R^{y}EHN-doo.   House for rent.

2127. Доска́ объявле́ний.
dah-SKAH ahb-yihv-L^{y}EH-n^{y}ee.   Public notices.

2128. Же́нский туале́т.
ZHEHN-sk^{y}ee too-ah-L^{y}EHT.   Women's room.

2129. Заво́д. *zah-VOHT.*   Factory.

2130. Зака́зано. *zah-KAH-zuh-nuh.*   Reserved.

**2131. Закры́то на [обе́д] [переучёт] [ремо́нт]
[санита́рный де́нь].**
zah-KRĬ-tuh nah-[ah-B^{y}EHT] [p^{y}ih-r^{y}ih-oo-CHOHNT]
[r^{y}ih-MOHNT] [suh-n^{y}ee-TAHR-nï＿ee d^{y}ehn^y].
Closed for [lunch] [inventory] [repairs] [cleaning].

**2132. Закры́то с восьми́ часо́в ве́чера до девяти́
часо́в утра́.**
zah-KRĬ-tuh svahs^y-M^{y}EE chih-SOHF V^{y}EH-chih-ruh
duh-d^{y}ih-v^{y}ih-T^{y}EE chih-SOHF oo-TRAH.
Closed from 8:00 P.M. to 9:00 A.M.

2133. Закры́то по воскресе́ньям и пра́здникам.
*zah-KRĬ-tuh puh-vuhs-kr^yih-S^yEHN^y-yuhm ee
PRAHZ-n^yee-kuhm.*
Closed on Sundays and holidays.

2134. Заку́ски.
zah-KOOS-k^yee. Refreshments (OR: Appetizers).

2135. За́л ожида́ния.
zahl ah-zhĭ-DAH-n^yee-yuh. Waiting room.

2136. За́нято. *ZAH-n^yih-tuh.* Occupied.

2137. Запасно́й вы́ход.
zuh-pahs-NOY VĬ-khuht. Emergency exit.

2138. Запреща́ется.
zuh-pr^yih-SHHAH-yiht-tsuh. (Is) forbidden.

2139. Звони́ть. *zvah-N^yEET^y.* Ring bell.

2140. Зде́сь продаётся.
zd^yehs^y pruh-dah-YOHT-tsuh. On sale here.

2141. Зоопа́рк. *zah-ah-PAHRK.* Zoo.

2142. Иди́те.
ee-D^yEE-t^yih. Walk (signal for pedestrians).

2143. Ка́сса.
KAHS-suh. Cashier (OR: Ticket office).

2144. Кафе́. *kah-FEH.* Café.

2145. Кла́дбище.
KLAHD-b^yee-shhuh. Cemetery.

2146. Кли́ника. *KL^yEE-n^yee-kuh.* Clinic.

2147. К метро́. *km^yih-TROH.* To the subway.

2148. Ко́мната ма́тери и ребёнка.
KOHM-nuh-tuh MAH-t^yih-r^yee ee r^yih-B^yOHN-kuh.
Nursery.

2149. К поездáм.   *kpuh-yih-ZDAHM.*   To the trains.

2150. К себé.
ksʸih-BʸEH.   Pull (LIT.: Toward yourself).

2151. К таксú.   *ktahk-SʸEE.*   To the taxis.

2152. Купáться воспрещáется.
koo-PAHT-tsuh vuhs-prʸih-SHHAH-yiht-tsuh.
No swimming.

2153. Курúтельная кóмната.
koo-RʸEE-tʸihlʸ-nuh-yuh KOHM-nuh-tuh.
Smoking room.

2154. Курúть запрещáется (OR: воспрещáется).
*koo-RʸEETʸ zuh-prʸih-SHHAH-yiht-tsuh (OR:
   vuhs-prʸih-SHHAH-yiht-tsuh).*   No smoking.

2155. Лéстницы.   *LʸEHS-nʸee-tsï.*   Stairs.

2156. Лúфт.   *lʸeeft.*   Elevator.

2157. Меблирóванные кóмнаты в арéнду.
*mʸih-blʸee-ROH-vuhn-nï-yih KOHM-nuh-tï
   vah-RʸEHN-doo.*
Furnished rooms for rent.

2158. Местá для пассажúров с детьмú и инвалúдов.
*mʸihs-TAH dlʸuh-puh-sah-ZHĬ-ruhf zdʸihtʸ-MʸEE ee
   een-vah-LʸEE-duhf.*
Seats for passengers with children and invalids.

2159. Милúция.   *mʸee-LʸEE-tsï-yuh.*   Police.

2160. Мужскóй туалéт.
moosh-SKOY too-ah-LʸEHT.   Men's room.

2161. Музéй рабóтает с 10 ч. до 18 ч.
*moo-ZʸEH_EE rah-BOH-tuh-yiht zdʸih-sʸih-TʸEE
   chih-SOHF duh-vuh-sʸihm-NAHT-tsuh-tʸee
   chih-SOHF.*
The museum is open from 10 A.M. to 6 P.M.

2162. Му́сор. *MOO-suhr.* Refuse.

2163. Нале́во. *nah-L^{y}EH-vuh.* To the left.

2164. Напра́во. *nah-PRAH-vuh.* To the right.

2165. Напрока́т. *nuh-prah-KAHT.* For hire.

2166. Не ве́шать объявле́ний.
n^{y}ih-V^{y}EH-shuht^y ahb-yihv-L^{y}EH-n^{y}ee.
Post no bills.

2167. Не высо́вываться.
n^{y}ih-vï-SOH-vï-vuht-tsuh. Do not lean out.

2168. Не купа́ться.
n^{y}ih-koo-PAHT-tsuh. No swimming.

2169. Не кури́ть. *n^{y}ih-koo-R^{y}EET^y.* No smoking.

2170. Не плева́ть. *n^{y}ih-pl^{y}ih-VAHT^y.* No spitting.

2171. Не прислоня́ться.
n^{y}ih-pr^{y}ee-slah-N^{y}AHT-tsuh.
Do not lean (on doors).

2172. Нет вхо́да. *n^{y}eht FKHOH-duh.* No entry.

2173. Нет вы́хода. *n^{y}eht VÏ-khuh-duh.* No exit.

2174. Нет перехо́да.
n^{y}eht p^{y}ih-r^{y}ih-KHOH-duh. No crossing.

2175. Не шуме́ть. *n^{y}ih-shoo-M^{y}EHT^y.* No noise.

2176. Объявле́ние.
ahb-yihv-L^{y}EH-n^{y}ee-yuh.
Notice (OR: Announcement).

2177. Окра́шено. *ah-KRAH-shuh-nuh.* Wet paint.

2178. Опа́сно. *ah-PAHS-nuh.* Danger.

2179. Остано́вка [авто́буса] [тролле́йбуса] [трамва́я].
ah-stah-NOHF-kuh [ahf-TOH-boo-suh]
[trah-L^{y}EH ‿ EE-boo-suh] [trahm-VAH-yuh].
[Bus] [trolleybus] [streetcar] stop.

2180. Осторо́жно. *ah-stah-ROHZH-nuh.* Careful.

2181. Отлёт. *aht-L^yOHT.* Departure (airplane).

2182. Отправле́ние.
aht-prahv-L^yEH-n^yee-yuh. Departure.

2183. От себя́.
aht-s^yih-B^yAH. Push (LIT.: Away from yourself).

2184. Па́спортный стол.
PAHS-puhrt-nï_ee stohl. Passport desk.

2185. Переры́в с 1 до 2 ч.
p^yih-r^yih-RÏF SHCHAH-soo dah-DVOOKH chih-SOHF.
Closed on break from 1:00 to 2:00.

2186. Перехо́д.
p^yih-r^yih-KHOHT.
Crosswalk (OR: Transfer to another line on subway).

2187. Пешехо́ды.
p^yih-shï-KHOH-dï. Pedestrians.

2188. Подзе́мный перехо́д.
pahd-Z^yEHM-nï_ee p^yih-r^yih-KHOT.
Underpass for pedestrians.

2189. По газо́нам ходи́ть воспреща́ется.
puh-gah-ZOH-nuhm khah-D^yEET^y vuhs-pr^yih-SHHAH-yiht-tsuh.
Keep off the grass.

2190. Поезда́ да́льнего сле́дования.
puh-yih-ZDAH DAHL^y-n^yuh-vuh SL^yEH-duh-vuh-n^yee-yuh.
Long-distance trains.

2191. Поликли́ника.
puh-l^yee-KL^yEE-n^yee-kuh. Outpatient clinic.

2192. Поса́дка. *pah-SAHT-kuh.* Boarding.

2193. Посторо́нним вхо́д запрещён.
puh-stah-ROHN-nʸeem vkhoht zuh-prʸih-SHHOHN.
No trespassing.

2194. По́чта (OR: **Почта́мт**).
POHCH-tuh (OR: *pahch-TAHMT*).   Post office.

2195. Почто́вый я́щик.
pahch-TOH-vĭ_ee YAH-shheek.   Postal box.

2196. Предвари́тельная прода́жа биле́тов.
*prʸihd-vah-RʸEE-tʸihlʸ-nuh-yuh prah-DAH-zhuh
bʸee-LʸEH-tuhf.*   Advance ticket sales.

2197. Прибы́тие. *prʸee-BĬ-tʸee-yuh.*   Arrival.

2198. При́городные поезда́.
PRʸEE-guh-ruhd-nĭ-yih puh-yih-ZDAH.
Suburban trains.

**2199. Приём и́ вы́дача [корреспонде́нции]
[перево́дов] [посы́лок].**
*prʸee-YOHM ee VĬ-duh-chuh [kuhr-rʸihs-pahn-DʸEHN-
tsi-yee] [pʸih-rʸih-VOH-duhf] [pah-SĬ-luhk].*
[Letters] [money orders] [parcels].

2200. Приёмные часы́ с 9 до 1 ч.
*prʸee-YOHM-nĭ-yih chih-SĬ zdʸih-vʸih-TʸEE
dah-CHAH-soo.*
Office hours: 9:00–1:00.

2201. Продаётся. *pruh-dah-YOHT-tsuh.*   For sale.

2202. Прода́жа биле́тов [на сего́дня].
prah-DAH-zhuh bʸee-LʸEH-tuhf [nuh-sʸih-VOHD-nʸuh].
Tickets on sale [for today].

2203. Прода́жа конве́ртов, ма́рок, откры́ток.
*prah-DAH-zhuh kahn-VʸEHR-tuhf, MAH-ruhk,
aht-KRĬ-tuhk.*
Envelopes, stamps, postcards on sale.

2204. Проезд воспрещён.
prah-YEHST vuhs-pr^yih-SHHOHN.
No thoroughfare.

2205. Просьба не курить.
PROHZ^y-buh n^yih-koo-R^yEET^y.　No smoking, please.

2206. Просят не кормить.
PROH-s^yuht n^yih-kahr-M^yEET^y.
Please do not feed (the animals).

2207. Раздевалка.
ruhz-d^yih-VAHL-kuh.　Checkroom.

2208. Размен (OR: **Разменная касса**).
rahz-M^yEHN (OR: *rahz-M^yEHN-nuh-yuh KAHS-suh*).
Change (into smaller denominations).

2209. Расписание [поездов] [самолётов].
ruhs-p^yee-SAH-n^yee-yuh [puh-yih-ZDOHF]
　[suh-mah-L^yOH-tuhf].
[Train] [Airplane] schedule.

2210. Ремонт.
r^yih-MOHNT.　Repairs (OR: Men working).

2211. Руками не трогать.
roo-KAH-m^yee n^yih-TROH-guht^y.　Do not touch.

2212. Самообслуживание.
suh-mah-ahp-SLOO-zhï-vuh-n^yee-yuh.
Self-service.

2213. Свободно.　*svah-BOHD-nuh.*　Vacant.

2214. Сеанс без перерыва.
s^yih-AHNS b^yihs-p^yih-r^yih-RÏ-vuh.
Showing without intermission.

2215. Сегодня нет спектакля.
s^yih-VOHD-n^yuh n^yeht sp^yihk-TAH-kl^yuh.
No performance today.

2216. С кондиционированным воздухом.
*skuhn-d*ʸ*ee-tsï-ah-N*ʸ*EE-ruh-vuhn-nïm VOHZ-doo-khum.*
Air-conditioned.

2217. Служебный вход.
sloo-ZHEHB-nï_ee vkhoht.   Employees' entrance.

2218. Соблюдайте тишину.
*suh-bl*ʸ*oo-DAH_EE-t*ʸ*ih t*ʸ*ee-shï-NOO.*   Silence.

2219. Справки (OR: **Справочное бюро**).
*SPRAHF-k*ʸ*ee* (OR: *SPRAH-vuhch-nuh-yuh b*ʸ*oo-ROH*).
Information (OR: Information office).

2220. Станция.   *STAHN-tsï-yuh.*   Railroad station.

2221. Стойте.
*STOY-t*ʸ*ih.*   Wait (signal for pedestrians).

2222. Стол заказан.
stohl zah-KAH-zuhn.   Table reserved.

2223. Столовая.
stah-LOH-vuh-yuh.   Dining room (OR: Cafeteria).

2224. Стоп-кран.   *stohp-krahn.*   Emergency brake.

2225. Стоянка такси.
*stah-YAHN-kuh tahk-S*ʸ*EE.*   Taxi stand.

2226. Ступайте осторожно.
*stoo-PAH_EE-t*ʸ*ih ah-stah-ROHZH-nuh.*
Watch your step.

2227. Телевидение.
*t*ʸ*ih-l*ʸ*ih-V*ʸ*EE-d*ʸ*ih-n*ʸ*ee-yuh.*   Television.

2228. Телевизор.
*t*ʸ*ih-l*ʸ*ih-V*ʸ*EE-zuhr.*   Television set.

2229. Телефон.   *t*ʸ*ih-l*ʸ*ih-FOHN.*   Telephone.

2230. Телефон-автомат.
*t*ʸ*ih-l*ʸ*ih-FOHN-ahf-tah-MAHT.*   Pay telephone.

2231. То́лько пешехо́ды.
TOHL^y-kuh p^yih-shï-KHOH-dï.   Pedestrians only.

2232. Туале́т (PL.: **Туале́ты**).
too-ah-L^yEHT (PL.: *too-ah-L^yEH-tï*).   Toilet.

2233. Убо́рщик (F.: **Убо́рщица**).
oo-BOHR-shheek (F.: *oo-BOHR-shhee-tsuh*).   Janitor.

2234. У на́с не ку́рят.
oo-NAHS n^yih-KOO-r^yuht.   No smoking.

2235. Фа́брика.   *FAH-br^yee-kuh*.   Factory.

2236. Холо́дная (вода́).
khah-LOHD-nuh-yuh (*vah-DAH*).   Cold (water).

2237. Убо́рная.   *oo-BOHR-nuh-yuh*.   Toilet.

INDEX

The phrases in this book are numbered consecutively from 1 to 2237. The entries in the index refer to those numbers. In addition, each major section heading (capitalized entries) is indexed according to page number. In cases where there may be confusion, parts of speech are indicated by the following abbreviations: *adj.* for adjective, *adv.* for adverb, *n.* for noun, *prep.* for preposition, and *v.* for verb. Parentheses are used for explanations, just as they are in the body of the phrasebook. Quotation marks are used to indicate Russian entries that are the functional rather than the lexical equivalents of an English entry; the Russian entry "цветы" under "florist (shop)" literally means "flowers," but is what you would be most likely to see on a shop sign.

Because of the already large extent of the indexed material, cross-indexing has generally been avoided. Phrases or groups of two words or more will generally be found under only one of their components (e.g., "express train" only under "express," though there is a separate entry for "train" alone). If you do not find a phrase under one of its words, try another.

Every English word or phrase in the index is followed by one or more Russian equivalents, which are ordinarily given in dictionary form (the nominative singular for nouns, the masculine nominative singular of adjectives, the nominative of pronouns, and the infinitive of verbs, except for participles, which are listed in their masculine nominative singular form). Feminine equivalents of masculine nouns follow the abbreviation F.

In effect, the reader is provided with a basic English-Russian glossary of up-to-date language. Of course, a knowledge of the Russian alphabet and an acquaintance with Russian grammar are essential for making the best use of this index, especially since Russian is a highly inflected language. To assist you in using the correct forms of words, the index lists all the sentences that include different forms of a word. Under "want" (infinitive хотéть), for example, sentences 62 and 147 are listed. They provide the forms хотíте (you [formal or plural] want) and хочý (I want), respectively. Invariable words are only indexed once, and only one appearance of each variation is listed, so that there are no duplicate listings. The beginner would do well to look at all the sentences listed for a Russian word in order to become familiar with the range of variations (and at all the Russian equivalents listed for an English word in order to become familiar with their different shades of meaning).

It is of course not the purpose of the present book to supply all the inflectional endings or to teach you Russian grammar. But it will give you the proper form to look up in a dictionary, where you will find further information.

Where a numbered sentence contains a choice of Russian equivalents (e.g., sentence 523, which gives пóчта and почтóвое отделéние for "post office"), only the first choice has been included in the index. (Always refer to the numbered sentence for more information.)